EFFICIENT ASSET MANAGEMENT

EFFICIENT ASSET MANAGEMENT

A Practical Guide to Stock Portfolio Optimization and Asset Allocation

Second Edition

By Richard O. Michaud and Robert O. Michaud

OXFORD
UNIVERSITY PRESS

2008

OXFORD
UNIVERSITY PRESS

Oxford University Press, Inc., publishes works that further
Oxford University's objective of excellence
in research, scholarship, and education.

Oxford New York
Auckland Cape Town Dar es Salaam Hong Kong Karachi
Kuala Lumpur Madrid Melbourne Mexico City Nairobi
New Delhi Shanghai Taipei Toronto

With offices in
Argentina Austria Brazil Chile Czech Republic France Greece
Guatemala Hungary Italy Japan Poland Portugal Singapore
South Korea Switzerland Thailand Turkey Ukraine Vietnam

Copyright © 2008 by Oxford University Press, Inc.

Published by Oxford University Press, Inc.
198 Madison Avenue, New York, New York 10016

www.oup.com

Oxford is a registered trademark of Oxford University Press.

Library of Congress Cataloging-in-Publication Data

Michaud, Richard O., 1941–
    Efficient asset management: a practical guide to stock portfolio optimization
    and asset allocation / Richard O. Michaud and Robert O. Michaud.—2nd ed.
        p. cm.—(Financial management association survey and synthesis series)
    Includes bibliographical references (p.) and index.
    ISBN 978-0-19-533191-2
    1. Investment analysis—Mathematical
    models. 2. Portfolio management—Mathematical models.
    I. Michaud, Robert O. \ II. Title.
    HG4529.M53 2008
    332.6—dc22 2007020912

9 8 7 6 5 4 3

Printed in the United States of America on acid-free paper

To

My mother, Helena Talbot Michaud, and her steadfast love
My father, Omer Michaud, and his cherished memory
Prof. Robin Esch, a wise, unerring mentor
Drs. Allan Pineda, John Levinson, and Cary Atkins

Richard Michaud, 2007

Preface

Effective asset management is not only a matter of identifying desirable investments: it also requires optimally structuring the assets within the portfolio. This is because the investment behavior of a portfolio is typically different from the assets in it. For example, the risk of a portfolio of U.S. equities is often half the average risk of the stocks in it.

Prudent investors concern themselves with portfolio risk and return. An understanding of efficient portfolio structure is essential for optimally managing the investment benefits of portfolios. Effective portfolio management reduces risk while enhancing return. For thoughtful investors, portfolio efficiency is no less important than estimating risk and return of assets.

Most institutional investors and financial economists acknowledge the investment benefits of efficient portfolio diversification. Optimally managing portfolio risk is an essential component of modern asset management. Markowitz (1959, 1987) gave the classic definition of portfolio optimality: a portfolio is efficient if it has the highest expected (mean or estimated) return for a given level of risk (variance) or, equivalently, least risk for a given level of expected return of all portfolios from a given universe of securities. Markowitz mean-variance (MV) efficiency is a practical and convenient framework for defining portfolio optimality and for constructing optimal stock portfolios and asset allocations. A number of commercial services provide optimizer software for computing MV efficient portfolios.

INVESTOR ACCEPTANCE

Modern asset management typically employs many theoretical financial concepts and advanced analytical techniques. Perhaps the most outstanding example is in the management of derivative instruments. Within a few years of the publication of seminal papers (Black & Scholes, 1973; Merton, 1973) and the opening of derivative exchanges, an extensive industry applying quantitative techniques to derivative strategies emerged. In a similar fashion, many fixed income managers use sophisticated portfolio structuring techniques for cash flow liability management.[1] In contrast, many institutional equity managers do not use MV optimizers to structure portfolios.

The relatively low level of analytical sophistication in the culture of institutional equity management is one often-cited reason for the lack of acceptance of MV optimization, along with organizational and political issues. The investment policy committee and an optimizer perform essentially the same integrative investment function. Consequently, the firm's senior investment officers may view an optimizer, and the quantitative specialist who manages it, as usurping their roles and challenging their control and political power in the organization.

Despite these reasons, it is hard to imagine why investment managers do not behave in their best interests as well as those of their clients. Experience in derivatives and fixed income management demonstrates that the investment community quickly adopts highly sophisticated analytics and computer technology when provably useful. If cultural, political, or competence factors limit the use of MV optimizers in traditional investment organizations, new firms should form without these limitations, with the objective of leveraging the technology and dominating the industry. Indeed, many "quantitative" equity management firms, formed over the past 35 years, have this objective. However, the "Markowitz optimization enigma"—the fact that many traditional equity managers ignore MV optimization—can be largely explained without recourse to irrationality, incompetence, or politics (Michaud, 1989a). The basic problem is that MV portfolio efficiency has fundamental investment limitations as a practical tool of asset management. It is likely that the limitations of MV optimizers have been an important factor in limiting the success of many quantitative equity managers relative to their more traditional competitors.

THE FUNDAMENTAL ISSUE

Although Markowitz efficiency is a convenient and useful theoretical framework for defining portfolio optimality, in practice it is a highly error-prone and unstable procedure that often results in "error maximized" and

---

1. Liebowitz (1986) describes some of these techniques.

"investment irrelevant" portfolios (Jobson & Korkie, 1980, 1981; Michaud, 1989a). Proposed alternative optimization technologies share similar, if not even more significant, limitations. MV efficiency limitations in practice generally derive from a lack of statistical understanding of the MV optimization process. A "statistical" view of MV optimization leads to new procedures that eliminate the most serious deficiencies for many practical applications. Statistical MV optimization may enhance investment value while providing a more intuitive framework for asset management. A statistical view also challenges and corrects many current practices for optimized portfolio management.

OVERVIEW

This book describes the problems associated with MV optimization as a practical tool of asset management and provides resolutions that reflect its essential, though often neglected, statistical character. A review of proposed alternatives of MV optimization is given and their theoretical and practical limitations are noted. A "statistical" perspective serves as a valuable route for the development and application of powerful techniques that enhance the practical value of MV optimized portfolios. The goal is to conserve the many benefits of traditional MV optimization while enhancing investment effectiveness and avoiding its rigidity. New tools are developed that enable an intuitive effective framework for meeting the demand characteristics from institutional asset managers to sophisticated financial advisors and investors. A simple asset allocation example illustrates the issues and new procedures. The text maintains a practical perspective throughout.

The second edition is extensively revised. Chapters 7 and 9 are nearly completely rewritten with new techniques, research, and expanded scope. Chapters 4, 5, 6, 8, 10, and 11 are extensively revised. The remaining chapters have also been updated.

The new reader will find a rich investment-practice–informed set of ideas, while the reader of the first edition will find extensive new material, including expansion of scope as well as development of earlier ideas. The new edition benefits from nearly 7 years of the authors' experience applying the technology to a wide spectrum of practical investment needs, including those of institutional asset managers, investment strategists, high-net-worth advisors, institutional consultants, and financial advisors worldwide. The authors also have nearly 3 years of actual asset management using the technology with favorable results.

FEATURES

This text is the first to integrate and systematically treat practical MV optimization from a statistical, rather than a numerical, point of view.

The focus is to enhance the investment value of MV optimized portfolios in asset management practice. The features include:

- The Resampled Efficient Frontier™ (REF):[2] REF optimized portfolios are provably effective at enhancing risk-adjusted performance. Implications of a more effective optimality on ineffective practices in contemporary asset management are discussed.
- Resampled Efficiency™ (RE) Rebalancing:[3] RE rebalancing provides statistically rigorous procedures for trading, monitoring, and asset importance analysis for practical management of MV optimized portfolios.
- Enhanced Index-Relative Optimization: New REF optimization techniques are presented for enhancing risk-adjusted performance of index-relative optimized and long-short portfolios, including new tools for large index management.
- Enhanced Liability-Relative Optimization: Discussion of economic liability modeling and REF optimization with applications to pension liability management.
- Improved Estimation: Neglected modern statistical techniques for improving the forecast value of historically estimated risk and return.
- Active Management Input Estimation: Bayes techniques for improving the investment value of active return.
- Comparison of Unconstrained and Linear Constrained MV Optimization: The discussion includes the serious limitations of MV optimization analytical formulas and the character of computational techniques.
- Optimization Design: Institutional techniques for managing investment information properly and avoiding optimization errors
- MV Optimization Review: Includes review of basic principles and limitations of alternative approaches.

PATENTS

The reader should note that various techniques and practices described within this book particularly in chapters 6, 7, and 9, are covered by the claims of patents, issued and pending, in the US and other countries, including US Patent Nos. 6,003,018 and 6,928,418. U.S. law provides that any use within the United States of a patented invention during the

---

2. REF optimization, invented by Richard Michaud and Robert Michaud, first described in Michaud (1998, Chapter 6), is protected by U.S. and Israeli patents and patents pending worldwide. New Frontier Advisors, LLC (NFA) is exclusive worldwide licensee.
3. RE rebalancing, invented by Robert Michaud and Richard Michaud, first described in its current form in Michaud and Michaud (2002), is protected by U.S. patents and patents pending worldwide. New Frontier Advisors, LLC (NFA) is exclusive worldwide licensee.

term of the patent and without the authority of the patent owner is an infringement of the patent, while corresponding provisions apply in other jurisdictions. Any party contemplating the use of a patented article or process, as defined by the claims of a patent, must obtain authorization of the patent owner before beginning any use. A request for permission to use the invention should specify, as completely as possible, the nature of the intended use.

DEMO OPTIMIZER

A CD that provides access to a demo Optimizer is included with the purchase of the book. It offers a limited-function version of the optimization and rebalancing procedures described in this book. When inserted into your CD drive, a pop-up window will appear to guide you in signing up for an account to run the software for a limited time. The Optimizer allows you to generate some exhibits similar to those in the book using the preloaded base case data described in Chapter 2. You are able to make changes with constraints and other assumptions to analyze their effects. You can also enter your own sample data set for experimenting with the RE optimizer and rebalancer. The Optimizer automatically compares the classical MV solution to the RE solution in tables and charts. The Optimizer software is provided for non-commercial educational uses only. All other applications are proscribed.

AUDIENCE AND ANALYTICAL REQUIREMENTS

Knowledge of statistical methods and modern finance at the level of a relatively nontechnical paper in the *Financial Analysts Journal, Journal of Investment Management,* or *Journal of Portfolio Management* is desirable. CFAs and MBAs should be well equipped to manage the material. The discussions are mostly self-contained and generally require little additional reading. The technical level required of the reader in the body of the text is relatively minimal. The footnotes and appendices discuss technical issues and topics of special interest. Experience in institutional asset management practice is a plus.

The primary audience for the text is institutional investment practitioners, sophisticated investors, investment strategists, financial advisors at various levels of sophistication, and academic and professional researchers in applied financial economics. Investors, investment managers, strategists, consultants, trustees, and brokers will be interested given the widespread use of MV portfolio construction and asset management techniques and the need to stay current in investment technology. Sophisticated financial advisors will have interest given the growing use of model portfolios and investment strategies for 401(k) investment and the need to understand portfolio construction and Exchange Traded Funds (ETF) investments. Academic and professional financial economists will have interest when using and understanding MV optimization. The book may be useful as a supplement in advanced undergraduate and graduate courses in investment management, in graduate courses in quantitative asset management, and for courses on portfolio optimization in institutional asset management.

ACKNOWLEDGMENTS

The second edition is most indebted to the research, interest, and ongoing support of Harry Markowitz. Our admiration of his towering body of work only increases as our understanding deepens. The second edition has benefited from the valuable support and interest of Gifford Fong, Olivier Ledoit, Andrew Lo, and Richard Roll. We heartily thank our associates at New Frontier Advisors, LLC for their ideas and encouragement, especially Matthew Pierce, Elise Schroeder, Allison Frankel, and Abigail Gabrielse, and comments and suggestions from our valued clients. A special thanks to Dan diBartolomeo, whose support was instrumental in the viability of our work. The second edition remains indebted to the revolutionary work of J. D. "Dave" Jobson and Bob Korkie on the statistical nature of MV efficiency. The first edition benefited from valuable discussions with Philippe Jorion and James L. Farrell, Jr. Neither edition would have appeared without the advice, encouragement, and early support of J. Peter Williamson, Philip Cooley, and Gary Bergstrom and his esteemed associates at Acadian Asset Management.

We are pleased to hear from readers. Please send your comments, questions, and corrections to our e-mail addresses rmichaud@newfrontieradvisors.com or romichaud@newfrontieradvisors.com, or visit our Web site at http://www.newfrontieradvisors.com for updates on research in optimized portfolio management and investment technology.

Contents

EFFICIENT ASSET MANAGEMENT

1

Introduction

MARKOWITZ EFFICIENCY

Markowitz (1959) mean-variance (MV) efficiency is the classic paradigm of modern finance for efficiently allocating capital among risky assets. Given estimates of expected return, standard deviation or variance, and correlation of return for a set of assets, MV efficiency provides the investor with an exact prescription for optimal allocation of capital. The Markowitz efficient frontier (Exhibit 1.1) represents all efficient portfolios in the sense that all other portfolios have less expected return for a given level of risk or, equivalently, more risk for a given level of expected return. In this framework, the variance or standard deviation of return defines portfolio risk. MV efficiency considers not only the risk and return of securities, but also their interrelationships.

Exhibit 1.1 illustrates these concepts: Portfolio A is assumed to be the investor's current portfolio, with a given expected return and standard deviation. Portfolio B is the efficient portfolio that has less risk at the same level of expected return of portfolio A. Portfolio C is the efficient portfolio that has more expected return at the same level of risk as portfolio A. The efficient frontier describes the mean and standard deviation of all efficient portfolios.

In most modern finance textbooks, MV efficiency is the criterion of choice for defining optimal portfolio structure and for rationalizing the value of diversification. Markowitz efficiency is also the basis for many important advances in positive financial economics. These include the Sharpe (1964)-Lintner (1965) capital asset pricing model

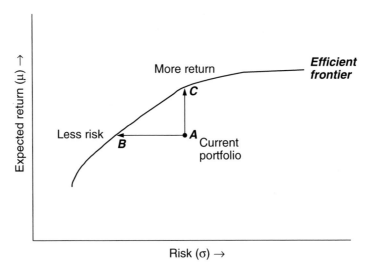

Exhibit 1.1 Mean Variance Portfolio Efficiency

(CAPM) and recognition of the fundamental dichotomy between systematic and diversifiable risk.

Many investment situations may use MV efficiency for wealth allocation. An international equity manager may want to find optimal asset allocations among international equity markets based on market index historic returns. A plan sponsor may want to find an optimal long-term investment policy for allocating among domestic and foreign bonds, equities, and other asset classes. A domestic equity manager may want to find the optimal equity portfolio based on forecasts of return and estimated risk. MV optimization is sufficiently flexible to consider various trading costs, institutional and client constraints, and desired levels of risk. In these cases, and in others, MV efficiency serves as the standard optimization framework for modern asset management.

AN ASSET MANAGEMENT TOOL

MV optimization is useful as an asset management tool for many applications, including:

1. Implementing investment objectives and constraints
2. Controlling the components of portfolio risk
3. Implementing the asset manager's investment philosophy, style, and market outlook
4. Efficiently using active return information (Sharpe, 1985)
5. Conveniently and efficiently imbedding new information into portfolios

TRADITIONAL OBJECTIONS

Academics and practitioners have raised a number of objections to MV efficiency as the appropriate framework for defining portfolio optimality. These "traditional" criticisms of MV efficiency tend to fall into one of the following categories:

1. *Investor Utility:* the limitations of representing investor utility and investment objectives with the mean and variance of return
2. *Normal Distribution:* the limitations of representing return with normal distribution parameters
3. *Multiperiod Framework:* the limitations of MV efficiency as a single-period framework for investors with long-term investment objectives, such as pension plans and endowment funds
4. *Asset-Liability Financial Planning:* claims that asset-liability simulation is a superior approach for asset allocation

Chapter 3 examines each category of objection in detail. These traditional objections often do not address the most serious limitations of MV optimizers, nor do they provide useful alternatives in many cases. On the other hand, the robustness of MV optimization is often unappreciated, and several workarounds make the MV framework useful in many situations of practical interest.

THE MOST IMPORTANT LIMITATIONS

In practice, the most important limitations of MV optimization are instability and ambiguity. MV optimizers function as a chaotic investment decision system. Small changes in input assumptions often imply large changes in the optimized portfolio. Consequently, portfolio optimality is often not well defined. The procedure overuses statistically estimated information and magnifies the impact of estimation errors. It is not simply a matter of garbage in, garbage out, but rather a molehill of garbage in, a mountain of garbage out. The result is that optimized portfolios are "error maximized" and often have little, if any, reliable investment value. Indeed, an equally weighted portfolio may often be substantially closer to true MV optimality than an optimized portfolio.

The frequent failure of optimized portfolios to meet practical investment objectives has led a number of sophisticated institutional investors to abandon the method for alternative procedures and to rely on intuition and priors. The limitations of MV optimization have also contributed to the lack of widespread acceptance of quantitative equity management. The problems of MV optimization are not easily resolved with alternative risk measures, objective functions, or simulation procedures: they are endemic to most optimization procedures.

RESOLVING THE LIMITATIONS OF MEAN-VARIANCE OPTIMIZATION

The problems of MV optimization instability and ambiguity are ultimately those of over-fitting data. Statistical estimates define an efficient frontier. Because of variability in the input estimates, many portfolios are statistically as efficient as the ones on the efficient frontier. In other words, an appropriate statistical test would not be able to differentiate the efficiency of many portfolios off the efficient frontier from those on it. A computation of "statistically equivalent" efficient portfolios[1] reveals the variability and essential statistical character of MV optimization. A statistical perspective helps to resolve many of the most serious practical limitations of MV optimization and is often associated with a significantly reduced need to trade.

Many of the most important methods for reducing the instability and ambiguity of the optimization process and enhancing its investment value are based on statistical procedures that have largely been ignored by the financial community. These techniques come from financial theory, econometrics, and institutional research and practice.

Practitioners may ignore procedures for enhancing MV optimization for a variety of reasons. The enormous prestige and goodwill that Markowitz and his work enjoy in the investment community have led many to ignore the obvious practical limitations of the procedure. Many influential consultants, software providers, and asset managers have vested commercial interests in the status quo. For others, practical considerations have hampered implementation. Until recently, some of the statistical techniques have been inconvenient or inaccessible because they required high-speed computers and advanced mathematical or statistical software. Finally, the statistical character of MV optimization requires a fundamental shift in the notion of portfolio optimality, the need to think statistically, and a significant change in procedures.

ILLUSTRATING THE TECHNIQUES

Asset allocations are important in their own right and provide a useful framework for analyzing many of the fundamental problems of optimization. A simple global asset allocation problem illustrates several of these issues and alternative procedures.

· The new methods presented in the following chapters can significantly reduce the impact of estimation errors, enhance the investment meaning of the results, provide an understanding of precision, and stabilize the optimization. In isolation, each procedure can be helpful; together, they may have a substantial impact on enhancing the investment value of optimized portfolios.

---

1. Chapter 7 provides procedures for defining statistical equivalent efficient portfolios.

2

Classic Mean-Variance Optimization

This chapter describes in relatively simple terms some of the essential technical issues that characterize MV optimization and portfolio efficiency. For the sake of compact discussion, the introduction of some basic assumptions and mathematical notation will be useful. An example of an asset allocation optimization illustrates the techniques presented here and throughout the text.

PORTFOLIO RISK AND RETURN

Suppose estimates of expected returns, variances or standard deviations, and correlations for a universe of assets.[1] The expected return, μ (mu), of a portfolio of assets P, μ_P, is the portfolio-weighted expected return for each asset.[2] The variance σ^2 (sigma squared) of a portfolio of assets P, σ_P^2, depends on the portfolio weights, the variance of the assets in the portfolio, and the correlation, ρ (rho), between pairs of assets.[3] The standard deviation σ is the square root of the variance and is a useful alternative

---

1. As noted below, the covariance can also define the optimization risk parameters.
2. Statisticians use the Greek letters μ and σ to represent mean and standard deviation. Let μ_i, $i = 1..N$, refer to the expected return for asset i in the N asset universe. Let w_i refer to the weight of asset i in portfolio P. The sum of portfolio weights w_i times the expected returns μ_i for each asset i in the universe is equal to the expected return for portfolio P. In mathematical notation, the symbol Σ_i denotes the summation from 1 to N and the portfolio expected return is defined as: $\mu_P = \Sigma_i w_i^* \mu_i$.
3. Following the notation above, the variance of portfolio P, σ_P^2, is the double sum of the product for all ordered pairs of assets of the portfolio weight for asset i, the portfolio weight for asset j, the standard deviation for asset i, the standard deviation for asset j, and the correlation between asset i and j. In mathematical notation, $\sigma_P^2 = \Sigma_i \Sigma_j w_i^* w_j^* \sigma_i^* \sigma_j^* \rho_{i,j}$, where σ is the standard deviation (square root of the variance) and ρ is the correlation. The quantity $\sigma_{i,j}$ is known as the covariance. It is equal to $\sigma_i^* \sigma_j^* \rho_{i,j}$

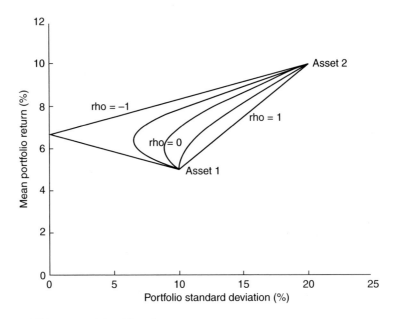

Exhibit 2.1 Portfolio Risk and Return: Two-Asset Case

for describing asset risk. One reason for preferring the standard deviation to the variance is that it is in the same units of return as the mean.

Exhibit 2.1 shows the mean and standard deviation for a portfolio consisting of two assets. It illustrates some essential properties of portfolio expected return and risk. Asset 1 has an expected return of 5% and risk of 10%, and asset 2 has an expected return of 10% and risk of 20%. Five curves connect the two assets and display the risk and expected return of portfolios, ranging from 100% of capital in asset 1 to 100% in asset 2. The asset correlations associated with the five curves (from right to left) are 1.0, 0.5, 0, –0.5, and –1.0.

The five curves illustrate how correlations and portfolio weights affect portfolio risk and expected return. When the correlation is 1, as in the extreme right-hand curve in the exhibit, portfolio risk and expected return is a weighted average of the risk and return of the two assets. In this case, there is no benefit to diversification. In all other cases, except for the assets themselves, portfolio risk is less than the weighted average of the risk of the assets. In most cases, asset correlations are less than 1. U.S. stock correlations are often within a 0.3 to 0.5 range. As the level of correlation diminishes, the amount of available risk reduction increases. In the case of a –1 correlation between two assets (the extreme left-hand curve), it is possible to eliminate portfolio risk.

---

and is often used as an alternate way to define the variance. The covariance matrix Σ consists of all ordered pairs of the covariances.

DEFINING MARKOWITZ EFFICIENCY

Exhibit 2.1 shows that an appropriate set of portfolio weights may significantly reduce portfolio risk in many cases. The notion of defining an optimal set of portfolio weights to optimize risk and return is the basis of Markowitz portfolio efficiency. The efficiency criterion states:

> A portfolio P* is MV efficient if it has least risk for a given level of portfolio expected return.[4]
>
> The MV efficiency criterion is equivalent to maximizing expected portfolio return for a given level of portfolio risk.
>
> A portfolio P* is MV efficient if it has the maximum expected return for a given level of portfolio risk.[5]

Which formulation of portfolio efficiency is used is a matter of convenience.

As Exhibit 1.1 indicates, each portfolio on the efficient frontier satisfies the efficiency criterion. The efficient frontier is monotonic increasing in the mean return as a function of increasing portfolio risk.

OPTIMIZATION CONSTRAINTS

Linear constraints are generally included in institutional MV portfolio optimization. For example, optimizations typically assume that portfolio weights sum to 1 (budget constraint)[6] and are nonnegative (no-short-selling constraint).[7] The budget condition is a linear equality constraint on the optimization. The no-short-selling condition is a set of sign constraints or linear inequalities (one for each asset in the optimization) and reflects avoidance of unlimited liability investment often required in institutional contexts. In practice, optimizations often include many additional linear inequality and equality constraints, particularly for equity portfolios.

The budget and no-short-selling constraints form a standard set of optimization constraints that are used in many of the optimization illustrations in the text. Recently, advances in trading technology have made short-selling strategies more economically viable. Long-short portfolio optimization may include several assets with bounded negative weight constraints. Long-short investing is addressed more specifically in Chapter 9. As will be shown, the statistical methods and innovations described in the text, properly implemented, also apply to long-short and leverage optimization strategies.

---

4. Formally, portfolio P* is MV efficient if, for any portfolio P, $\mu_P = \mu_{P*}$ implies $\sigma_P^2 \geq \sigma_{P*}^2$.
5. Formally, portfolio P* is MV efficient if, for any portfolio P, $\sigma_P^2 = \sigma_{P*}^2$ implies $\mu_P \leq \mu_{P*}$.
6. In mathematical notation, the budget constraint implies that $\sum_i w_i = 1$.
7. In mathematical notation, $w_i \geq 0$, for all portfolio assets.

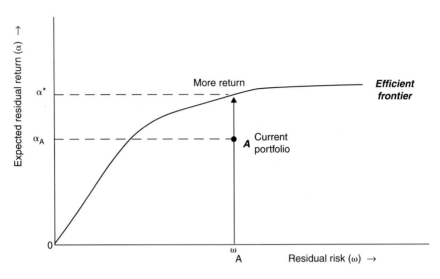

Exhibit 2.2 Residual Risk and Return Portfolio Efficiency

THE RESIDUAL RISK-RETURN EFFICIENT FRONTIER

A variation of classic Markowitz MV efficiency called benchmark optimization is based on "residual" return. (Given an appropriate benchmark, the difference between asset and benchmark return defines residual return.) It is convenient to use the following notation for MV residual return efficiency. Let:

α = expected residual return
ω^2 = residual return variance.

The definition of Markowitz efficiency for residual return is precisely the same as before, with α and ω replacing μ and σ.

By definition, the benchmark has zero expected residual return and residual risk. In many applications, a portfolio, such as an index, defines the benchmark. Exhibit 2.2 illustrates the notion of MV residual return efficiency. In this case, an investor with portfolio A wants to optimize expected residual return at the same level of residual risk. The exhibit assumes that the benchmark return is a feasible portfolio. The efficient frontier is the collection of all portfolios with maximum α for all possible levels of portfolio residual risk.

COMPUTER ALGORITHMS

Several methods are available for estimating MV efficient portfolios. The method used may depend on the constraints. For example, an MV optimization that includes only linear equality constraints, such as the budget constraint, can be solved analytically with matrix algebra similar to a linear regression.[8] On the other hand, an MV optimization that includes linear inequality constraints requires numerical analysis procedures for solution.

"Quadratic programming" is the technical term for the numerical analysis procedure used to compute MV efficient portfolios in practice. Quadratic programming algorithms allow maximization of expected return and minimization of the variance, subject to linear equality and inequality constraints. The term *quadratic* refers to the variance in the optimization objective; *programming* refers to optimizations that include linear inequality as well as equality constraints.

Many algorithms are used for computing MV efficient portfolios. The choice may depend on convenience, computational speed, number of assets, number and character of constraints, and required accuracy. Various tradeoffs govern the choice of algorithm for a given problem.[9] The optimization examples in this and following chapters use an exact quadratic programming procedure.[10]

ASSET ALLOCATION VERSUS EQUITY PORTFOLIO OPTIMIZATION

Asset allocation and equity portfolio optimization are the two typical applications of MV optimization in asset management. In both cases the optimization finds optimal allocations of capital to maximize expected return and minimize risk subject to various constraints. The underlying optimization issues in both cases are those illustrated in Exhibits 1.1 or 2.2. There are, however, some noteworthy differences between asset allocation and equity portfolio optimization.

In an asset allocation study, the number of risky assets rarely exceeds 50 and is typically in the range of 5 to 20. The number of optimization constraints are often little more than budget and sign constraints. The assets generally include broad asset categories, such as U.S. equities and corporate and government bonds, international equities and bonds, real estate, hedge funds, and venture capital. Sample means, variances, and correlations, based on monthly, quarterly, or annual historic data, may serve as starting points for optimization input estimates.[11] In a benchmark-relative framework such as that shown in Exhibit 2.2, the residual return basis for optimization inputs is the difference between asset and index returns.

8. For example, Alexander and Francis (1986) and Jobson and Korkie (1985). Optimization with only a budget constraint is addressed in Chapter 4.
9. See the appendix.
10. Computer algorithms that include linear constraints as in Markowitz (1956) are used to compute practical MV optimal portfolios. See Boyd and Vandenberghe (2004) for an up-to-date review of algorithms for solving convex optimization problems including Markowitz portfolio optimization.
11. See Chapters 8 and 11 for further discussion of input estimation.

For equity portfolio management, benchmark optimization (see Exhibit 2.2) is generally the framework of choice. This is true because the measure of investment performance for institutional equity management is almost always benchmark-relative. The benchmark return is usually related to the return of a representative market index.

An equity portfolio optimization generally includes many securities. Domestic equity optimizations typically include 100 to 500 stocks. International equity optimizations may include as many as 4,000 to 10,000 stocks. Equity portfolio optimizations usually include many constraints on portfolio characteristics, industry or sector membership, and trading cost restrictions.

The source of equity optimization inputs is normally very different from those in an asset allocation. Sample means and covariances of historic returns are typically not the starting points for inputs in an equity portfolio optimization. Modern financial theory provides a rich framework for defining expected and residual return for equities.[12] In equilibrium, the expected return of a security is a function of its systematic risk. High expected return may indicate high systematic risk and not mispricing. The estimate of expected return associated with systematic risk generally derives from some version of the capital asset pricing model or arbitrage pricing theory.[13]

Equity risk models provide useful estimates of the components of stock and portfolio residual risk shown in Exhibit 2.2. In practice, institutional asset managers often use commercial risk measurement services to estimate security and portfolio residual risk. Over- and under-pricing is associated with α, or expected return net of systematic risk adjusted expected return. The process of defining α for equity portfolio optimization is often a major undertaking and may be the primary investment focus of an equity management firm. Many institutional asset managers employ stock valuation procedures based on sophisticated econometric analysis and techniques.[14]

Another common application of MV optimizers for equity portfolio management is to define a tracking or index fund.[15] In this case, α is zero and the optimizer finds the minimum risk-tracking portfolio given the constraints. Without constraints or trading costs, the minimum tracking fund is the index. For tracking funds, the efficient frontier in Exhibit 2.2 reduces to a point on the x-axis near or at the origin.

For equity portfolios, estimation of α and security and portfolio residual risk, portfolio constraints, trading costs, the number of assets, and other issues of practical importance substantially increase the

12. The two most influential modern financial theories of stock pricing are the Sharpe (1964)-Lintner (1965) capital asset pricing model (CAPM) and the Ross (1975, 1976) arbitrage pricing theory (APT).
13. Commercial services may use a compromise version of an "expanded" or multi-beta CAPM that is similar to an APT framework to define systematic risk.
14. For a recent example see Michaud (1999).
15. An index fund is a portfolio designed to track an index. One simple method for defining an index fund is to include all the stocks in the index with index weights as portfolio weights. In this case, optimization is not required. Optimizers may be useful when constraints are required or liquidity issues are important.

Table 2.1 Monthly Net Dollar Returns (Percentages), January 1978–December 1995

	Euro Bonds	US Bonds	Canada	France	Germany	Japan	UK	US
Mean	0.83	0.85	0.97	1.46	1.11	1.46	1.37	1.29
Standard Deviation	1.99	1.52	5.47	7.00	6.19	7.01	5.99	4.28

Note: U.S. 30-Day T-Bill Return: Mean = 0.58, Standard Deviation = 0.24.

complexity of the optimization process. In contrast, asset allocation typically reflects a much simpler and pedagogically convenient framework for the study of MV optimization.

A GLOBAL ASSET ALLOCATION EXAMPLE

Consider a global asset manager allocating capital to the following eight major asset classes: U.S. stocks and government/corporate bonds, Euro bonds, and the Canadian, French, German, Japanese, and U.K. equity markets. The historic data consists of 216 months, from January 1978 through December 1995, of index total returns in U.S. dollars for all eight asset classes and for U.S. 30-day T-bills, from January 1978 through December 1995.[16] Table 2.1 provides the averages and standard deviations of the monthly data for the assets in this period.[17]

Quadratic programming finds the optimal MV efficient frontier asset allocations under the assumptions. Exhibit 2.3 displays the efficient frontier for the usual constraints.[18] The graph displays annualized data.[19] The exhibit includes plots and labels of the means and standard deviations of the eight assets.

16. The data for the five equity markets—Canada, France, Germany, Japan, United Kingdom—are Morgan Stanley Capital International U.S. dollar total return indices net of withholding taxes. The U.S. equity data are S&P 500 Index total returns. The 30-day T-bill returns are from Salomon Brothers. The two bond data indices are the Lehman Brothers government/corporate U.S bond indices and U.S. dollar Eurobond global indices. The Lehman Brothers Eurobond Global Index was available from January 1978 to November 1994. The Eurobond returns for the remaining months were from Lehman Bros. Eurobond Global Issues Index. The limited availability of long-term Eurobond returns governed the choice of time period used in this example.

17. These assets make up the base case used throughout this book and featured in the demo Optimizer as the book data.

18. Computing and displaying the efficient frontier in Exhibit 2.3, and in subsequent examples of efficient frontiers, means computing and displaying a set of points representing the mean and standard deviation of a representative set of efficient portfolios. The procedure used computes 51 efficient portfolios, ranging from minimum variance to maximum expected return portfolios. A step function straight-line fills in between the computed points to graphically display the efficient frontier. In general, the points chosen are equally spaced along the return axis of the efficient frontier.

19. Twelve multiplies the average monthly returns, and the square root of 12 multiplies the monthly return standard deviations.

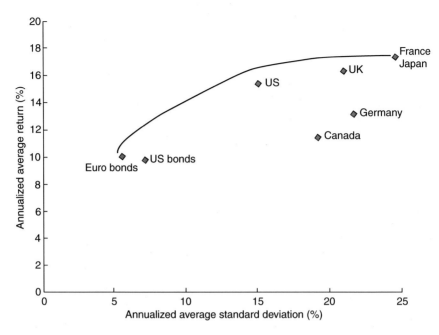

Exhibit 2.3 Classical Mean-Variance Efficient Frontier

Because the French stock market index had the highest average monthly return, it is on the efficient frontier at the most northeast point of the curve. The Japanese market had nearly the same return and risk, and its plot in Exhibit 2.3 is nearly indistinguishable from that of France. The minimum risk portfolio is more than 98% Euro bonds, with 0.86% average monthly return and 1.52% monthly standard deviation. Other points on the efficient frontier lie between these two extremes. For example, the efficient frontier asset allocation with average monthly return 1.24% and standard deviation 3.33% (roughly halfway between the largest and smallest return efficient portfolios) is composed of approximately 10% French, 20% Japanese, 5% U.K., and 45% U.S. equities and 20% Euro bonds. U.S. bonds significantly underperformed all other assets and an efficient portfolio for its level of risk. In Exhibit 2.3, it is clear that the French, Japanese, United Kingdom, and U.S. equity markets as well as Euro bonds are near or on the efficient frontier and performed well relative to their level of risk in this time period. For many levels of risk, however, diversification was useful.

REFERENCE PORTFOLIOS AND PORTFOLIO ANALYSIS

Reference portfolios are often helpful in understanding the investment meaning of efficient frontiers. They serve as useful guideposts for

Table 2.2 Reference Portfolio Composition (%)

	Euro Bonds	US Bonds	Canada	France	Germany	Japan	UK	US
Index	0	0	5	10	10	30	10	35
Current	5	20	5	10	5	20	15	20
Equal	12.5	12.5	12.5	12.5	12.5	12.5	12.5	12.5

comparing the implications of alternative portfolios. Table 2.2 defines three reference portfolios used in subsequent analyses of MV portfolio efficiency: index, current, and equal weighted. The index portfolio is roughly consistent with a capitalization-weighted portfolio devoid of bonds relative to a world equity benchmark for the six equity markets. The current portfolio represents a typical U.S.-based investor's global portfolio asset allocation. The most significant differences between the index and current portfolios are the allocations to fixed income assets. An equal-weighted portfolio is useful as a reference point.

Exhibit 2.4 provides the results of including the reference portfolios in the efficient frontier analysis. All the reference portfolios plot close to the efficient frontier and appear reasonably well diversified.

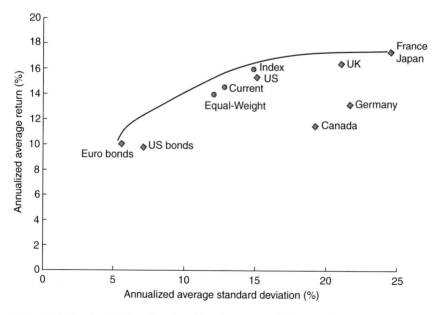

Exhibit 2.4 Classical Efficient Frontier with Reference Portfolios

RETURN PREMIUM EFFICIENT FRONTIERS

The return premium is the return minus the risk-free rate. It is often convenient to use total return premiums, instead of total returns, as the basis of MV analysis in practice. Return premiums are similar to real rates of return. By removing the impact of varying risk-free rates, return premiums may be relatively more stable than total returns and more useful in a forecasting context.

The total return premium is the U.S. dollar total return minus the U.S. dollar short-term interest rate in each period. The monthly short-term interest rate for a U.S. dollar-based investor is usually defined as the U. S. T-bill 30-day return. Table 2.3 displays the mean and standard deviation of the total monthly return premiums over the January 1978 to December 1995 period for the eight assets in Table 2.1. Table 2.4 provides the correlations. The data in tables 2.3 and 2.4 give a complete description of the input parameters required for MV optimization.

Exhibit 2.5 displays the MV efficient frontier associated with the historic return premium data. Exhibit 2.5 and tables 2.3 and 2.4 are the basis of most of the examples illustrated in the text.

Table 2.3 Monthly Dollar (Net) Return Premium Returns (Percentages), January 1978–December 1995

	Euro Bonds	US Bonds	Canada	France	Germany	Japan	UK	US
Mean	0.27	0.25	0.39	0.88	0.53	0.88	0.79	0.71
Standard Deviation	1.56	2.01	5.50	7.03	6.22	7.04	6.01	4.30

Table 2.4 Asset Correlations Monthly Dollar (Net) Return Premium Returns (Percentages) January 1978–December 1995

	Euro Bonds	US Bonds	Canada	France	Germany	Japan	UK	US
Euro Bonds	1.00	0.92	0.33	0.26	0.28	0.16	0.29	0.42
US Bonds	0.92	1.00	0.26	0.22	0.27	0.14	0.25	0.36
Canada	0.33	0.26	1.00	0.41	0.30	0.25	0.58	0.71
France	0.26	0.22	0.41	1.00	0.62	0.42	0.54	0.44
Germany	0.28	0.27	0.30	0.62	1.00	0.35	0.48	0.34
Japan	0.16	0.14	0.25	0.42	0.35	1.00	0.40	0.22
UK	0.29	0.25	0.58	0.54	0.48	0.40	1.00	0.56
US	0.42	0.36	0.71	0.44	0.34	0.22	0.56	1.00

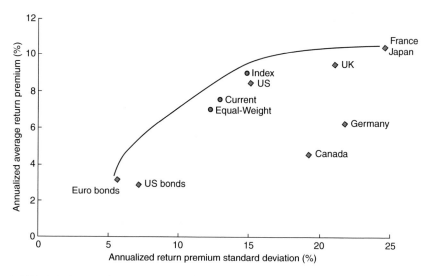

Exhibit 2.5 Mean-Variance Return Premium Efficient Frontier

APPENDIX: MATHEMATICAL FORMULATION OF MV EFFICIENCY

Mean-Variance Efficiency

Let:

N = number of assets or securities in the universe

w = vector of portfolio weights of the N assets

μ = vector of expected returns of the N assets

Σ = covariance matrix of the N assets

$\mathbf{1}$ = vector of ones of length N

By definition, the mean and variance of a portfolio P with weights w_P is:

$$\mu_P = w_P' * \mu$$
$$\sigma_P^2 = w_P' * \Sigma * w_P$$

where w' denotes the transpose of the vector w.

If portfolio P is MV efficient for a given level of portfolio expected return μ^*, then it satisfies the following conditions:

minimize: $w_P' * \Sigma * w_P$

subject to the constraint: $w_P' * \mu = \mu^*$.

In many cases of practical interest, portfolio weights are further constrained to sum to 1,

$$w_P' * \mathbf{1} = 1$$

and to have non-negative values $\quad w \geq 0$.

Parametric Quadratic Programming and MV Efficiency

"Parametric" quadratic programming is a useful alternative formulation of MV efficiency. In this case, a parameter λ (lambda) is introduced into the description of the optimization. The condition that identifies the efficient portfolios is to minimize ϕ (phi):

$$\phi = \sigma_P^2 - \lambda\, \mu_P$$

for a given value of λ subject to the associated linear equality and inequality constraints. This formulation of MV optimization leads to efficient computation of the entire MV efficient frontier.[20]

To show how this works, it is convenient to introduce the concept of a "pivot point" or "corner portfolio" on the efficient frontier. Technically, corner portfolios are efficient frontier portfolios that represent transition points where at least one of the inequalities in the optimization either becomes binding or is no longer binding on the solution. Less technically, a corner portfolio is an efficient portfolio in which an asset either enters or leaves the set of efficient portfolios in a neighborhood of the corner portfolio.[21]

Corner portfolios are important for computing the efficient frontier due to the following technical property: if w^* and w^{**} are vectors representing weights of portfolios on the efficient frontier, then a portfolio formed from the convex sum of the two portfolios—$c^*w^* + (1-c)^*w^{**}$, $0 < c < 1$—is also an MV efficient portfolio if no corner portfolio exists between w^* and w^{**}. Consequently, the efficient frontier between w^* and w^{**} is computable simply from knowing the composition of two distinct efficient portfolios, when corner portfolios do not exist between them. Parametric quadratic procedures find the values of λ associated with the corner portfolios. It is therefore possible to compute all corner portfolios and thereby the entire efficient frontier exactly and efficiently using parametric quadratic programming methods. This approach is often more efficient than simply computing a large number of portfolios across the length of the efficient frontier.

Parametric quadratic programming is conceptually interesting because it provides a deeper understanding of the nature of the MV efficient frontier. In many practical applications, however, computing efficient portfolios at specific values of portfolio expected return or risk is often of primary interest, and parametric quadratic programming of the efficient frontier is not needed.

---

20. Early parametric quadratic programming methods include the critical-line algorithm of Markowitz (1956) and Beale (1955). For an extensive up-to-date discussion of the critical-line algorithm see Markowitz (1987). Computational methods based on the simplex algorithm include Beale (1959), Frank and Wolfe (1956), and Wolfe (1959). See Boyd and Vandenberghe (2004) for an up-to-date review of algorithms for solving convex optimization problems including Markowitz portfolio optimization.
21. See Sharpe (1970) for a more leisurely exposition.

Exact Versus Approximate MV Optimizers

In the past MV optimization algorithm design depended on tradeoffs of computational speed versus accuracy required.[22] This was particularly true for equity portfolio optimizations for large stock universes with many constraints. Enhancements such as Perold (1984) were valuable for large-scale optimization problems in the presence of factor models. However, recent developments in computational power and algorithmic sophistication have largely eliminated the need for approximate optimization algorithms even for large international equity portfolios.[23]

22. Readers may be surprised to know that many commercial asset allocators as well as equity portfolio optimizers are not exact solution algorithms. Approximate algorithms have limitations not only for inaccurate estimation but also for finding solutions when none may exist.
23. Currently and near term, computer laptop technology features multi-core processors that allow extremely fast optimization for even large problems.

3

Traditional Criticisms and Alternatives

Many authors have raised objections to mean-variance (MV) efficiency as a framework for defining portfolio optimality. Most of the alternatives can be classified in one of five categories: (1) alternative risk measures; (2) utility function optimization; (3) multiperiod objectives; (4) Monte Carlo financial planning; and (5) linear programming. Analysis shows that the alternatives often have their own serious limitations and that MV efficiency is far more robust than is commonly appreciated. Although they are symptomatic of an underlying unease with MV efficiency, none of the proposals address the basic limitations of MV optimization.

ALTERNATIVE MEASURES OF RISK

In MV efficiency, the variance, or standard deviation, of return is the measure of security and portfolio risk. The variance measures variability above and below the mean. From an investor's point of view, the variance of returns above the mean is often not viewed as "risk". One obvious and intuitively appealing nonvariance measure of risk, discussed as early as Markowitz (1959), is the semivariance or semistandard deviation of return. In this risk measure, only returns below the mean are included in the estimate of variability.

The semivariance is an example of a "downside" risk measure. In this case, "downside" risk is relative to the average or mean of return. There are many other ways to measure "downside" risk. A simple example is replacing average return with a specified level of return, such as zero or the risk-free rate.

Many other nonvariance measures of variability are also available. Some of the more important include the mean absolute deviation and range measures. The pros and cons of various risk measures depend on the nature of the return distribution.

The return distribution of an asset or portfolio depends on several factors. Because the returns of diversified equity portfolios, equity indexes, and other assets are often approximately symmetric over periods of institutional interest, efficiency based on nonvariance risk measures may be nearly equivalent to MV efficiency.

An important issue is whether, in practice, nonvariance risk measures lead to significantly different efficient portfolios. Exhibit 3.1 provides an illustration, comparing the MV efficient frontier in Exhibit 2.5 with a mean-semivariance efficient frontier based on the same historic data. As Exhibit 3.1 shows, the two efficient frontiers are virtually identical, except in the middle. The differences in the middle reflect the fact that some equity indices have asymmetrically less downside risk. Many currently fashionable risk alternatives have similar efficient frontier characteristics.

Some securities, such as options, swaps, hedge funds, and private equity, have return distributions that are unlikely to be symmetric. The return distributions of fixed-income and real estate indices are generally less symmetric than equity indices. In addition, the return distribution of diversified equity portfolios becomes increasingly asymmetric over long time horizons. Consequently, the variance measure for defining portfolio efficiency is not always useful or appropriate. For many applications of institutional interest, however, a variance-based efficient frontier is often little different (and even less often statistically significantly different) from frontiers that use other measures of risk.[1]

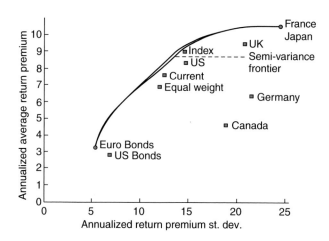

Exhibit 3.1 MV and Semi-Variance Return Premium Efficient Frontiers

1. We turn to measures of statistically significant difference in Chapter 7.

A word of caution: alternative risk measures are often more difficult to estimate accurately. Analysts must weigh the trade-off between estimation error and a more conceptually appealing measure of risk.

Most importantly, the appropriate risk measure is not one based on historic return distributions but on how an investor understands the risk that will be borne in the investment period. As a forecast, many distribution parameters are realistically unanticipatable in direction as well as magnitude relative to the level of uncertainty associated with investment. Consequently, as a measure of future risk, the variance is often perfectly adequate to represent investor risk perceptions even for highly asymmetric return indices and assets.

UTILITY FUNCTION OPTIMIZATION

For many practicing financial economists, maximum expected utility of terminal wealth is the framework of choice for all rational decision making under uncertainty. If Markowitz MV efficiency is not consistent with expected utility maximization, perhaps it should be abandoned and replaced with utility function optimization.

Markowitz MV efficiency is strictly consistent with expected utility maximization only under either of two conditions: normally distributed asset returns or quadratic utility. The normal distribution assumption is unacceptable as a realistic hypothesis. Although diversified equity portfolio and capital market index returns are often reasonably symmetric, their distribution is not normal.[2] In addition, the limitations of quadratic utility as a representation of investor behavior are well known and unacceptable.[3] Consequently, MV efficiency is not strictly consistent with expected utility maximization.

On the other hand, there are significant practical limitations to using utility functions as the basis of defining an optimization. One obvious limitation is the feasibility and viability of practical algorithms for computing optimal portfolios. Depending on functional form, nonlinear optimization methods may be required that may have significant limitations in many applications.

An equally important limitation of the utility function approach to portfolio optimization is utility function specificity. In practice, investor utility is unknown. The lack of specificity of the investor's utility function is a far more daunting practical problem than it may appear. This

2. Returns are neither strictly normal nor log-normal. Returns are not normal due to limited liability. Returns are not log-normal due to the possibility of default. Financial history includes many extended time periods when even country capital markets stopped functioning.
3. Because a quadratic function is not monotone increasing as a function of wealth, from some point on, expected quadratic utility declines as a function of increasing wealth. Quadratic utility functions are primarily useful as approximations of expected utility maximization in some region of the wealth spectrum.

is because a class of utility functions can have similar functional forms, perhaps differing in the value of only one or two parameters, yet represent a very wide, even contradictory, spectrum of risk bearing and investment behavior (Rubinstein, 1973). In these cases, even small errors in the estimation of utility function parameters can lead to very large changes in the investment characteristics of an optimal portfolio. As a practical matter, the problem of specifying with sufficient accuracy the appropriate utility function for a given investor appears to be a severe practical limitation of utility function-based portfolio optimization.

The practical resolution is to consider Markowitz MV efficiency as a convenient approximation of expected utility maximization. A quadratic utility is often a useful approximation of maximum expected utility at a point for almost any reasonable utility function and return-generating process in practice.[4] Note that the best-approximating quadratic function is simply some two-moment approximation of maximum expected utility that is a function of utility parameters. Consequently, MV efficient portfolios are often good approximations of maximum expected utility and a practical framework for portfolio optimization (Kroll, Levy, & Markowitz 1984; Levy & Markowitz, 1979; Markowitz, 1987, chapter 3).

The use of utility functions in defining portfolio optimality often divides practitioners from academics. From a rigorous academic point of view, only the specification of an appropriate utility function will do for defining portfolio optimality. However, few practitioners use nonquadratic utility functions to find optimal portfolios. Given the difficulty of estimating utility functions with sufficient precision, the convenience of quadratic programming algorithms, and the robustness of the approximating power of quadratic utility at a point, MV efficiency is often the practical tool of choice.

MULTIPERIOD INVESTMENT HORIZONS

Markowitz MV efficiency is formally a single-period model for investment behavior. Many institutional investors, however, such as endowment and pension funds, have long-term investment horizons on the order of 5, 10, or 20 years. How useful is MV efficiency for investors with long-term investment objectives?

One way to address long-term objectives is to base MV efficiency analysis on long-term units of time. MV efficiency, however, is probably most appropriate for relatively short-term periods. This is true because a quadratic approximation of maximum expected utility is most likely to be valid for relatively short time horizons such as monthly, quarterly, or yearly periods. In addition, lengthening the unit of time reduces the number of independent periods in a historic data set and the statistical

---

4. The result is Taylor's theorem for a continuous and sufficiently smooth utility function.

significance of optimization parameter estimates. On the other hand, increasing the historic data period may diminish the relevance of the estimates for the forecast period.

An alternative approach is to consider the multiperiod distribution of the geometric mean of return. The geometric mean, or compound, return is the statistic of choice for summarizing portfolio return over multiple periods.[5]

Assume that, in each period, MV efficiency defines optimal portfolio choice. Also assume that the distribution of single-period return does not vary (appreciably) over the multiperiod investment horizon. What are the long-term consequences of repeatedly investing in MV efficient portfolios?

Some essential results are due to Markowitz (1959, chapter 6). He shows that (1) MV efficient portfolios need not be efficient in the long run and (2) long-term efficiency is not necessarily monotonic in portfolio risk. In particular, MV efficient portfolios on the upper segment of the efficient frontier may be less efficient in the long term than portfolios with less risk.[6]

Hakansson (1971a) gives an example of an MV efficient frontier in which repeated investing produces a negative long-term geometric mean at all points. This example demonstrates that every portfolio on an MV efficient frontier may lead to ruin with probability 1 over a sufficiently long investment horizon. However, the Hakansson frontier is neither typical nor likely.

Further analysis of the geometric mean criterion is useful.[7] The mean and variance of N-period geometric mean return is a natural N-period generalization of Markowitz efficiency.[8] Various approximations show that portfolios on the (single-period) MV efficient frontier are often good approximations of N-period geometric mean efficient portfolios.[9] Consequently, N-period geometric mean MV efficiency is roughly a special case of MV efficiency in many cases of practical interest.

Define the critical point as the MV efficient portfolio with the maximum N-period expected geometric mean return. The critical point is a useful construct for understanding and using N-period geometric mean efficiency. The N-period expected geometric mean is a positive function of

---

5. Suppose an investor experiences a 100% return in one period and a –50% return in the next period. The two-period average return is 25%, but the two-period wealth is the same as at the beginning. Therefore, the true multiperiod return is 0%. The geometric mean provides the correct answer, while the average does not.

6. Markowitz's use of the phrases "return in the long-run" and "long-term return" refer to the almost sure limit of geometric mean return as the number of periods becomes large.

7. Much of the following discussion follows Michaud (1981, 2003).

8. It may be fitting to call the objective Hakansson efficiency, after the researcher who has done much of the pioneering work in this area.

9. For example, Young and Trent (1969) and Michaud (1981, appendix). Approximation accuracy depends on assumptions that are often satisfied in practical applications.

the mean of (single-period) expected return and a negative function of the variance. Consequently, the critical point defines the boundary of portfolios on the lower segment of the MV efficient frontier that are N-period geometric mean MV efficient and those on the upper segment that are not. N-period horizon MV efficiency leads to the simple decision rule of considering only MV efficient portfolios on the lower segment of the efficient frontier up to the critical point efficient portfolio.[10] Note that critical points that are not end points of the MV efficient frontier do not always exist.

A number of analysts have raised objections to the geometric mean as an investment criterion. In particular, a significant controversy emerged from the proposal of using the (long-term) expected geometric mean as a surrogate for expected utility (Hakansson, 1971b). This controversy, although it is beyond the scope of this discussion, is essentially concerned with the limitations of using any investment rule, however attractive, as an alternative to expected utility maximization. The opposing view concerns the limitations of using utility functions in practice and the value of the MV geometric mean criterion as a convenient source of useful investment information.[11] MV geometric mean investment objectives are often consistent with many institutional investment mandates.

One more issue may be of interest. The assumption has been that the investor repeatedly invests in the same efficient frontier portfolio over some investment horizon. However, optimal multiperiod investment with a MV geometric mean objective is a dynamic programming strategy that implies varying the choices of MV efficient portfolios in each period (Michaud & Monahan, 1981).

Multiperiod considerations are important issues for investors with long-term investment objectives. To avoid possible negative long-term consequences of MV efficiency, a simple solution is to limit consideration to efficient frontier portfolios at or below the critical point. As a useful approximation, it is convenient to consider long-term efficient portfolios as a subset and a special case of MV efficiency.

ASSET-LIABILITY FINANCIAL PLANNING STUDIES

Many financial institutions invest substantial resources in defining an appropriate long-term average asset allocation or investment policy.[12] They do this because the long-term average asset allocation is one of the most important investment decisions an institution or investor can

---

10. One simple procedure is to find the MV efficient portfolio with the maximum value of an MV approximation to the N-period geometric mean using a search algorithm of all portfolios on the efficient frontier. Michaud (1981) provides three analytic formulas for estimating the efficient frontier critical point for the special case of portfolios on the capital asset pricing model (CAPM) market line.
11. See Markowitz (1976), Michaud (1981, 2003) for further discussion and many additional references.
12. Such projects can involve a number of consultants and substantial expenditures.

make.[13] The importance of defining an optimal investment policy has spurred alternative approaches to defining portfolio optimality. Probably the most important is asset-liability financial planning based on Monte Carlo simulation of portfolio return and changing liabilities.

In a Monte Carlo financial planning study, a computer model simulates the random functioning of fund values and changes in liabilities over time.[14] Performing many Monte Carlo simulations results in estimates of possible cash flows and funding status over time. By varying asset return and asset allocation assumptions, the simulation can evaluate the implications of risk policy decisions on the evolution of funding status and cash flows. Endowment fund simulations can provide useful information on likely levels of endowment spending and fund value over time. Similarly, defined benefit pension plan simulations can be useful for anticipating required contributions and plan funding status for various assumptions and investment periods.[15]

The issue of interest is whether Monte Carlo asset-liability financial planning is a superior alternative to MV efficiency for defining an optimal asset allocation. Proponents argue that plan funding status and cash flow objectives are more meaningful than the MV efficiency of a feasible portfolio. The anticipation of likely cash flows and required contributions can provide valuable fund planning information. The problem is that such information may have relatively limited usefulness for defining an optimal long-term asset allocation.

Generally, only feasible MV efficient frontier asset allocations are likely to be of investment interest. This is because feasible allocations with more expected return for a given risk level are almost always preferable. Consequently, a valid Monte Carlo asset-liability simulation study generally requires MV efficiency analysis to determine candidate efficient allocations. Within the context of feasible efficient allocations, consider the consequences of varying asset mixes. In general, the Monte Carlo results show that riskier efficient asset mixes lead to a greater likelihood of meeting or exceeding funding objectives and of increasing volatility. Evaluating the trade-offs associated with funding status and cash flow volatility in various time periods is often of no less difficulty than evaluating the risk-return tradeoffs in an efficient frontier context. Monte Carlo

13. Brinson et al. (1986, 1991) have shown that the average risk level or long-term investment policy of the fund may account for more than 90% of investment results for long-term investors. Hensel et al. (1991) use a different definition of investment policy and find that it is roughly comparable to active asset allocation and active stock selection. At a minimum, most analysts agree that investment policy is at least as important as any other class of investment decisions.

14. Depending on the study and application, the liability model may be very detailed. For a defined benefit plan, it can include a comprehensive examination of corporate objectives, economic projections, and future hiring policy as well as current workforce census. In some cases, liability modeling may affect asset allocation decisions in terms of feasibility, particularly for regulated firms such as insurance companies.

15. Michaud (1976) provides a detailed example of the Monte Carlo financial planning process for defined benefit pension plans.

simulation studies do little more than illustrate the principle that, for feasible efficient portfolios, more risk leads to more return on average and more volatility, leaving the investor to choose what is most appropriate.

There is an exception to these basic principles governing Monte Carlo asset-liability financial planning simulation. Analysts have seen that increasing efficient portfolio risk does not always lead to increased average return. Such results appear to rationalize the importance of the Monte Carlo procedure relative to MV efficiency analysis. However, the discussion in the previous section can help to explain this result.

Monte Carlo simulation studies generally assume repeated investment in MV efficient frontier portfolios. If an efficient frontier has an internal critical point, efficient asset allocations on the long-term inefficient segment of the efficient frontier will exhibit the behavior that increasing risk leads to decreases in the ability of the fund to meet objectives. In many cases, such results can be anticipated analytically by computing the critical point of the efficient frontier and analyzing N-period geometric mean efficiency. However, the issue is more than simply a tool for rationalizing the results of a simulation study. The N-period geometric mean implications of asset return assumptions are the engine that drives the simulations and can lead to predefined conclusions.

Monte Carlo asset-liability simulation has many uses as a tool for financial planning. It is useful for understanding the likelihood of meeting funding objectives and likely cash flows associated with various fund investments and allocations. The procedure has limited value, however, as an alternative to MV efficiency for defining an optimal asset allocation. Many of its asset allocation benefits are analytically anticipatable in terms of the mean and variance of the multiperiod geometric mean distribution. On the other hand, the analytic tools for understanding the geometric mean distribution as a function of the MV efficient frontier portfolios over an N-period investment horizon can be useful for designing effective Monte Carlo simulation financial planning studies (Michaud, 1981, 2003).

LINEAR PROGRAMMING OPTIMIZATION

The limitations of MV optimization as a practical tool of equity portfolio management have been familiar to many astute asset managers for many years. One alternative is to optimize portfolios with linear programming.[16]

Linear programming portfolio optimization is a special case of quadratic programming. The most significant difference is that linear programming does not include portfolio variance. In this procedure, the objective is to maximize expected equity portfolio return subject to a variety of linear

---

16. See for example Farrell (1983, pp. 168–174).

equality and inequality constraints on portfolio structure. The procedure relies on clever use of constraints on industries, sectors, and stock weights to control portfolio risk and maximize expected return. The constraints also serve to design portfolios with various specific characteristics and objectives.

In the hands of a sophisticated analyst, linear programming is an optimization technique that may avoid some of the fundamental limitations of equity portfolio MV optimization. It has its own limitations, however. In practice, it is difficult to control the structure of a portfolio precisely. From a theoretical point of view, only an MV optimization framework can optimally use active forecast information (Sharpe, 1985). Given the current state of the art in optimization, linear programming can't be recommended. The problems of ambiguity and instability characteristic of MV optimization are well addressed in the statistical optimization framework that is a primary subject of this text.

A somewhat obvious final issue may be worthy of note. A number of investment institutions use surprisingly unsophisticated optimization procedures. These "homemade" optimization alternatives are often not the product of a conscious effort to avoid MV optimizer limitations but reflect a lack of analytical sophistication in the organization. Technical limitations in an optimization algorithm are unlikely to enhance the investment value of a portfolio over standard procedures.

4

Unbounded MV Portfolio Efficiency

Theoretical academic and practitioner research on MV optimization typically assumes an unbounded asset weight framework.[1] In this context a budget or asset sum-to-one constraint is all that is assumed, and uncertainty in risk-return estimates is ignored. The benefit of this framework is that MV optimization can be solved using analytical methods.[2] Elegant mathematical solutions and simple formulas are available for many questions of interest. The unbounded MV optimization framework has useful pedagogical applications. However, in investment practice, risk-return estimates are highly uncertain. As will be shown, avoiding the investment consequences of data uncertainty in unbounded MV optimization comes at the high price of irrelevant and/or misleading conclusions.[3] This chapter focuses on the fundamental limitations of unbounded MV efficiency for practical investment management when estimate uncertainty is considered and provides a context for many of the tools that follow.

---

1. A number of academic examples are reviewed in DeMiguel et al. (2006). Additional examples of theoretical MV optimization in the unbounded MV optimization framework include Black and Litterman (1992), Grinold (1989), Knight and Satchell (2006), and Clarke et al. (2002).
2. Portfolio optimization based on expected utility maximization ignoring uncertainty in data typically represents a similar class of problems with similar consequences for out-of-sample performance.
3. It is beyond the scope of the text to address the practical limitations of expected utility-based portfolio optimization without estimate uncertainty due to the wide range of possible utility functions considered in theoretical finance. Nevertheless, we note that the practical limitations are very similar to those we describe for MV optimization.

UNBOUNDED MV OPTIMIZATION

The formula for the optimal portfolio for unbounded MV optimization is:

$$x = \Sigma^{-1}\mu / (1' \, \Sigma^{-1}\mu) \tag{4.1}$$

where

Σ	is the covariance matrix.
Σ^{-1}	is the inverse covariance matrix.
μ	is the column vector of estimated returns.
x	is the column vector of optimal portfolio weights.
1	represents a column vector of ones with length equal to the number of assets.

Formula 4.1 for the optimal portfolio weights is easily solved with modern computer technology.[4] The optimal portfolio found from the formula is the maximum Sharpe ratio (return/risk) portfolio. It is also convenient to compute the minimum variance portfolio.[5] For the data in Chapter 2, Tables 2.3 and 2.4, Table 4.1 displays the solutions for the optimal asset weights. The Sharpe ratio for the maximum Sharpe ratio portfolio is 0.253 monthly or 0.876 annualized.[6]

Exhibit 4.1 describes the efficient set of risky unbounded MV efficient portfolios. All the portfolios on the MV efficient frontier are linear combinations of the maximum Sharpe ratio portfolio and the minimum variance efficient portfolios.[7] The display indicates the positions of the maximum Sharpe ratio, minimum variance, and equal weighted portfolios. Since there are no limitations on leverage or lending in the optimization, the set of portfolios on the unbounded efficient frontier may extend below the minimum variance portfolio and beyond the maximum Sharpe ratio portfolio.[8]

The optimal asset allocations in Table 4.1 may surprise readers unfamiliar with unbounded MV optimization. Large negative (short) and positive (more than 100% leveraged) positions typically characterize unbounded

Table 4.1 Optimal Unbounded MV Portfolio: Chapter 2 Data (Annualized) Percentages

Portfolio	US Bonds	Euro Bonds	Canada	France	Germany	Japan	UK	US
Max Sharpe Ratio	−86.5	163.8	−20.6	4.2	−4.5	8.6	6.9	28.1
Min Variance	−66.2	168.8	−1.1	−1.3	0.2	1.8	0.1	−2.3

4. The covariance matrix is assumed positive semi-definite.
5. The minimum variance portfolio is computed from $\Sigma^{-1}1/(1' \, \Sigma^{-1} 1)$ subject to the budget constraint.
6. Note that the Sharpe ratios reported in Michaud (1998, p. 35) are monthly.
7. Any two portfolios on the efficient frontier will allow tracing of the efficient frontier.
8. In an investment sense the portfolios below the minimum variance portfolio are not MV efficient but are nevertheless interestingly related to the efficient portfolios.

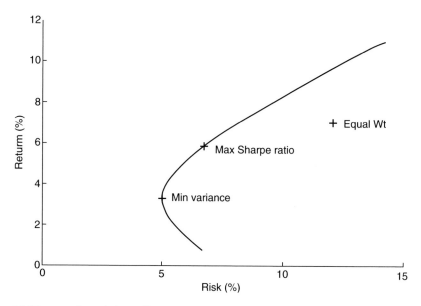

Exhibit 4.1 Unbounded MV Efficient Frontier (Chapter 2 Data)

MV optimization. The large negative and positive optimal portfolio weights are often impractical investments for even the largest financial institutions.

In the unbounded MV framework, essentially only one portfolio is of investment interest: the maximum Sharpe ratio portfolio. If a riskless asset exists, the efficient set consists of borrowing or lending the max Sharpe ratio portfolio at the riskless asset rate.[9]

THE FUNDAMENTAL LIMITATIONS OF UNBOUNDED MV EFFICIENCY

Optimizers are numerical algorithms that are insensitive to uncertainty in risk-return estimates. Modern computers assume numerical accuracy to 16 decimal places.[10] A return estimate of 10% is represented internally by the computer with 15 following zeros after the decimal point. Sixteen decimal places of accuracy is an absurdly unrealistic level of certainty for most investment information. Unfortunately, MV optimization is highly sensitive to even small changes in risk and return estimates. Anecdotally, investment practitioners are well aware of the instability of MV optimized portfolios. The operative question is not whether MV optimizations are unstable, unintuitive, ambiguous, and poorly performing but rather, how serious is the problem? In most cases, the problem is very serious indeed.

9. Markowitz (2005) shows that removing the assumption that the leveraging and lending rates are equal has important theoretical implications for market equilibrium.
10. The IEEE 754 digital computer standard implies data storage of essentially 10 single- or 16 double-precision decimals of floating point data. The authors use double-precision software for computation.

J.D. Jobson and Bob Korkie wrote the classic pioneering studies on the limitations of unbounded MV optimized portfolios. Jobson and Korkie (1980) made analytic estimates of the biases produced by MV optimizers when information is uncertain. They found that the biases in MV optimized portfolios can be very large. Jobson and Korkie (1981) used Monte Carlo resampling techniques to simulate the behavior of an unbounded MV optimizer.[11] For a given set of historic return data for 20 stocks and a 60-month estimation period, they found that the simulated MV efficient frontiers had an average maximum Sharpe ratio of 0.08.[12] This result contrasts with the true Sharpe ratio for the data (0.32) and the Sharpe ratio of an equal-weighted portfolio (0.27). The Jobson and Korkie results put to rest the fallacy that MV optimized portfolios are somehow better than others even though they are difficult to understand. MV optimized portfolios are hard to understand because they often do not make investment sense and do not have any useful investment value.[13]

REPEATING JOBSON AND KORKIE

To provide a baseline for the results that follow, it is useful to repeat the Jobson and Korkie experiment for the data in Tables 2.3 and 2.4.[14,15]

11. The Jobson and Korkie Monte Carlo simulation experiment is an example of data resampling or bootstrapping. Data resampling and bootstrapping methods have become increasingly important in modern statistics. Judge et al. (1988, pp. 416–419) provide an overview and Efron and Tibshirani (1993) a comprehensive authoritative description. One important reason that simulation is so useful is that it represents an out-of-sample test of the investment performance of MV optimized portfolios for the data and optimization assumptions. Alternative methods generally have to deal with the additional issue of changes in the underlying return distribution.

12. Jobson and Korkie's (1981) Monte Carlo simulation procedure is as follows. A set of means, standard deviations, and correlations of monthly returns for 20 stocks, estimated over some historic period, is assumed to be the true state of nature. Monte Carlo simulations of the historic data simulate 60- or 100-month returns for each asset. From the simulated returns, compute the simulated optimization inputs—means, standard deviations, and correlations of the 20 stocks—and associated efficient frontier maximum Sharpe ratio portfolios. Repeat this procedure many times. Because the simulated data have statistical error, each simulated efficient frontier is unlikely to be the true efficient frontier, and the estimated maximum Sharpe ratio portfolio varies with each simulation. Now compare the average Sharpe ratio for the simulated maximum Sharpe ratio portfolios to the actual maximum Sharpe ratio and the Sharpe ratio of an equal-weighted portfolio for the historic data.

13. Jobson and Korkie are not alone in noting the lack of investment value of unbounded MV optimization in practice. DeMiguel et al. (2006) test the performance of 14 models in the context of unbounded MV optimization and estimation error and find, as in Jobson and Korkie, that none are reliable improvements over equal weighting.

14. Jobson and Korkie (1981) use the following formula for computing the simulated maximum Sharpe ratio portfolios: smean*inv(scov), where smean is the row vector for the Monte Carlo simulated means and inv(scov) is the inverse of the simulated covariance matrix. The reward-to-risk ratio using the means and covariances of tables 2.3 and 2.4 is the measure of the performance of the simulated Sharpe ratio optimal portfolios. The simulated portfolios in this case are not short-selling-constrained. The simulated portfolios produced by the formula are unlikely to satisfy the budget constraint. Dividing the portfolio weights by their sum normalizes the portfolio so that it satisfies the budget constraint. However, the reward-to-risk ratio before and after normalization may be different if the sum of the weights is negative. The alternative used here is to ignore simulated portfolios when the sum of the weights is negative.

15. The simulated returns are multivariate normally distributed. The algorithm used in the results reported is mvnrnd.m from MathWorks. Tests using nonparametric (bootstrapping) and parametric (multivariate normal) resampling found results that were essentially the same.

As noted earlier, the true maximum (monthly) Sharpe ratio for our data is 0.253. Replicating the 216-month historical estimation period of the data, the average of the Sharpe ratios for 500 simulations of the eight-asset data is 0.200.[16] This value is 20% less than the true value.

Jobson and Korkie use 100- and 60-month estimation periods. Replicating Jobson and Korkie with 500 simulations and the eight-asset data, the average Sharpe ratio for 100 estimation periods is 0.157 and for 60 periods is 0.128.[17] The results show that shorter estimation periods have a significant impact on increasing estimation error and reducing the average performance of optimized portfolios, all other things being the same. There are three reasons why our simulations find less serious negative results for average out-of-sample investment performance: (1) lower variance diversified asset classes; (2) longer historic estimation period; and (3) smaller number of assets in the optimization universe.

IMPLICATIONS OF JOBSON AND KORKIE ANALYSIS

The results of the Jobson and Korkie studies should be sobering for investors. This is because the Jobson and Korkie simulation framework measures best, not worst, cases for MV portfolio optimization performance. Each simulated efficient frontier uses risk and return estimates that statistically represent the truth. In addition, the underlying return generating process is assumed to be stationary in the Jobson and Korkie tests. In practice, asset managers have no idea if their estimates represent, even approximately, an investment truth about the future. As importantly, the return generating process is not stationary in practice but varies over time. Neither of these additional sources of investment error are included in the Jobson and Korkie framework. These Jobson and Korkie "best case" results provide little, if any, comfort that unbounded MV optimization is useful in investment practice. As we will show, the lure of elegant analytical solutions promised by unbounded MV optimization will often lead to irrelevant and misleading conclusions.

MV optimization is an error-prone framework. The unrealistic level of estimate accuracy assumed by the computer in an MV optimization typically leads to investment irrelevant solutions unless highly constrained. In-sample utility function optimization studies that do not consider estimation error and out-of-sample performance have similar character and

---

16. The distribution of the reward-to-risk ratios of the simulated portfolios is of investment interest. The 5th percentile maximum Sharpe ratio is 0.138, the 95th percentile is 0.238, the minimum value is 0.088, and the maximum value is 0.248. The Sharpe ratios have a skew value of –1.08, indicating that when error maximization negatively affects the optimized portfolio, the effect may be very serious. The relatively large skew value is a function of the small number of assets in the example. Larger numbers of assets lead to less skew in the distribution of the maximum Sharpe ratios, all other things being equal.

17. The reported numbers are an average of the results of four 500 resampled simulations. There was negligible variance in the estimates.

practical investment limitations.[18] Out-of-sample performance simulation studies, as pioneered by Jobson and Korkie, offer a reliable route to understanding the investment value of portfolio optimization procedures.

Some limitations of Jobson and Korkie's results for institutional asset management should be noted. Optimized institutional portfolios generally include bounds on asset weights. For example, optimized portfolios are typically sign constrained. As demonstrated in the next chapter, sign constraints may significantly enhance the performance of MV optimized portfolios. Typical institutional portfolio optimization practices may moderate, but do not invalidate, the Jobson and Korkie results. Jobson and Korkie's results indicate the importance of imposing financially meaningful constraints on the optimization process when available.[19]

STATISTICAL MV EFFICIENCY AND IMPLICATIONS[20]

The pioneering studies of Jobson and Korkie demonstrate that unbounded MV optimization has essentially no practical investment value. Yet many authors, attracted by the elegance of analytical results, persist in ignoring estimation error and use the unbounded MV optimization framework for deriving investment laws[21] and rules of asset management[22] and recommend procedures for defining optimality.[23] However, estimation error severely limits any practical investment value that can be derived from unbounded MV optimization analysis. Conclusions derived from analytical solutions are likely to be unreliable or misleading.[24]

Effective portfolio optimization needs to consider uncertainty in investment information. The importance of estimation error in asset management practice is far more important than has been appreciated by much of the investment community. Ignoring the statistical nature of MV efficiency leads to counterproductive and suboptimal investment practices. On the other hand, recognition of the statistical character of MV optimization can lead to procedures that allow significant improvement of performance and tools for asset management.

---

18. An example of a utility function study relative to portfolio optimization is Chopra and Ziemba (1993). They claim that estimation error is more important in the return than the variance or correlation dimension. The framework they use is the effect of estimation error on in-sample expected utility rather than out-of-sample performance. The results in Chapter 6 demonstrate the fallacy of their conclusion and the importance of dealing with estimation error in both risk and return for defining investment-effective optimized portfolios in practice.

19. This is the recommendation in Frost and Savarino (1988).

20. One of the earliest mentions of the efficient frontier as a sample statistic is in Roll (1979).

21. Grinold (1989)

22. Grinold and Kahn (1994, Ch. 6), Clarke et al. (2002, 2006)

23. Black and Litterman (1992), Knight and Satchell (2006)

24. Michaud and Michaud (2005b)

5

Linear Constrained MV Efficiency

Chapter 4 addressed unbounded MV optimization. Elegant analytical solutions are available in this case. In investment practice, however, MV optimized portfolios include linear (inequality and equality) constrained asset weights. Linear constrained, not unbounded, MV optimization is typically the framework of choice for asset management in practice. Linear inequality constraints reflect the fact that asset managers have practical limits to shorting and leverage of investments.

When linear inequality constraints are included, the analytical methods associated with unbounded MV optimization are unavailable; computational methods are the only feasible solution. Markowitz (1956) recognized the importance of this distinction and provided a computational algorithm for solving linear constrained MV optimized portfolios. In this and following chapters we pursue the implications of estimation error for the practical investment framework of linear constrained MV portfolio efficiency.

LINEAR CONSTRAINTS

In practice, portfolio optimizations typically include many linear inequality and equality constraints. In particular, the plethora of constraints that typifies institutional MV equity portfolio optimization in much practice is often so extreme as to all but define the "optimal" portfolio. The simplest nontrivial linear constrained MV optimization of interest includes a budget and nonnegative inequality constraints on assets. The efficient frontier in Exhibit 2.5, using data from tables 2.3 and 2.4, assumes sign constraints on assets and the sum-to-one budget constraint. This is our base case in the text.[1]

It is of interest to compare the characteristics of the linear constrained MV efficient frontier to the unbounded case. Table 5.1 displays the optimal maximum Sharpe ratio and minimum variance portfolios for the Exhibit 2.5 efficient frontier base case. The max Sharpe ratio for the linear constrained MV efficient frontier is 0.216 monthly (0.75 annualized) as compared to 0.253 monthly (0.876 annualized) for the unbounded case. Comparing the optimized portfolios in Table 5.1 relative to Table 4.1 highlights the differences between the inequality constrained and unconstrained optimized solutions.

From a conceptual point of view, imposing constraints on an optimization may seem arbitrary and counterproductive. Constraints reduce in-sample return and/or risk of portfolios on the efficient frontier. However, it would be hard to rationalize why asset managers consistently use constraints in constructing portfolios that are likely to be counterproductive. Intuitively, managers use constraints to improve risk-return efficiency in the investment period, not reduce it.

The paradox of the presence of many optimization constraints in investment practice is easily reconciled when estimation error is considered. An unconstrained MV optimization significantly overweights (underweights) those securities that have large (small) estimated returns, negative (positive) correlations, and small (large) variances. These securities are, of course, the ones most likely to have large estimation errors. The error maximization effect creates unintuitive extreme allocation MV optimized portfolios.[2] The MV optimizer overuses information available in investment data. Constraints reduce the ability of MV optimizers to misuse extreme information. Indeed, Frost and Savarino (1988) show that the performance of sign-constrained MV optimized portfolios is enhanced on average. Chapter 6 further addresses performance issues.

Table 5.1 Optimal Linear Constrained MV Portfolio: Base Case (Annualized)

Portfolio	US Bonds	Euro Bonds	Canada	France	Germany	Japan	UK	US
Max Sharpe Ratio	0.0%	67.8%	0.0%	2.6%	0.0%	9.7%	1.7%	18.2%
Min Variance	0.0%	98.7%	0.0%	0.0%	0.0%	1.3%	0.0%	0.0%

1. This is the efficient frontier displayed in Exhibit 2.5.
2. It is not always easy to see the unintuitive investment character of MV optimized portfolios in equity portfolio optimizations due to the typically large number of securities in the optimization universe. However, classical MV optimized asset allocations that typically include a relatively small number of assets and are not severely constrained are usually found to be inconsistent with the investment intuition of experienced investors.

EFFICIENT FRONTIER VARIANCE

Does the efficient frontier have a variance?[3] At first blush the question may seem frivolous: How can curves have a variance? On reflection, however, the question is less obviously frivolous. An MV efficient frontier is based on statistically estimated parameters. Because different estimates may be statistically equivalent, the MV efficient frontier must have a variance. The operative question is how to estimate the variance. Analytical solutions are available for the variance of an unbounded MV efficient frontier (Jobson, 1991).

To estimate the variance of a linear constrained MV efficient frontier, use the Jobson and Korkie resampling procedure to compute "statistically equivalent" frontiers from optimization inputs. The collection of resampled statistically equivalent efficient frontiers demonstrates the variability implicit in efficient frontier estimation. For the efficient frontier in Exhibit 2.5, the data resampling simulation proceeds as follows:

1. Monte Carlo simulate 18 years of monthly returns based on the data in Tables 2.3 and 2.4 for the eight asset classes.
2. Compute optimization input parameters from the simulated return data.
3. Compute efficient frontier portfolios that satisfy the same constraints as those in Exhibit 2.5.[4]
4. Repeat steps 1 through 3 a large number of times.[5] By definition, each simulated efficient frontier is statistically equivalent to the efficient frontier in Exhibit 2.5.

Exhibit 5.1 displays the original Exhibit 2.5 efficient frontier in solid black and 25 gray statistically equivalent efficient frontiers.[6]

The character of the simulated efficient frontiers in Exhibit 5.1 may surprise many. The simulations clearly show that estimation error in both the risk and return dimensions strongly affects MV optimality ambiguity. Note the range of risk displayed in the simulated efficient frontiers. Some resampled efficient frontiers extend only half the range of risk of the original frontier, while others have substantially more risk. Less surprising, perhaps, is the very wide range of return observed in the resampled frontiers. While the original frontier returns range from 3% to 11%, the simulated efficient frontier returns range from 0% to 35%.[7] MV optimality ambiguity is a serious fact of life even for a small number

---

3. Unless otherwise stated, we assume in the following that the efficient frontier is linear constrained.
4. As described in Chapter 2, the procedure computes 51 efficient portfolios ranging from minimum variance to the maximum expected return portfolios, all satisfying base case constraint assumptions.
5. Unless otherwise noted, the simulations that follow assume 500 efficient frontier replications.
6. The display includes only 25 (out of 500) simulated MV efficient frontiers in order for the reader to be able to explicitly observe the characteristics of individual efficient frontiers resulting from the resampling process.
7. A greater number of simulations increases the range of efficient frontier risk and return observed.

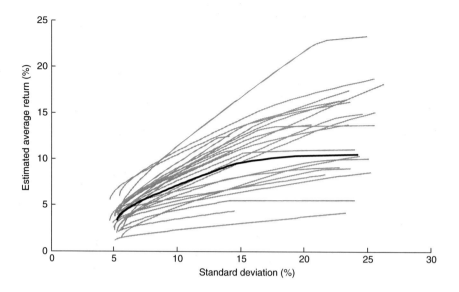

Exhibit 5.1 Original and 25 Resampled MV Efficient Frontiers

of very well diversified assets estimated over nearly a 20-year historic period.

Each simulated MV efficient frontier consists of 51 portfolios equally spaced along the return dimension from minimum to maximum value. Evaluate the mean and standard deviation of each of the simulated efficient frontier portfolios on each simulated efficient frontier relative to the risk-return inputs in tables 2.3 and 2.4. The area populated by the simulated efficient frontier portfolios below the classical MV efficient frontier displayed in Exhibit 5.2 heuristically describes a "statistical equivalence" region of alternative portfolios. The results consist of plotting the 51 portfolios from each simulated efficient frontier for 500 simulated efficient frontiers.[8]

The simulated efficient frontier portfolios computed from the simulated efficient frontiers in Exhibit 5.1 never plot above the original efficient frontier. If variability did not exist, the simulated efficient frontiers would be the same as Exhibit 2.5. To the extent that variability exists, the simulated efficient frontier portfolios vary from those in Exhibit 2.5 and plot below the original efficient frontier.[9]

Exhibits 5.1 and 5.2 dramatically illustrate the enormous, even startling, variability implicit in efficient frontier portfolio estimation. Very

8. The concept of the "statistical equivalence" region, discussed in Michaud (1989a), has important antecedents in the work of Jobson and Korkie (1981). Also, see Jobson (1991) and Jorion (1992).
9. This exercise is essentially the same as that in Jorion (1992).

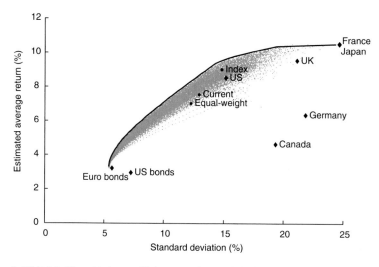

Exhibit 5.2 Mean-Variance Efficient Frontier Statistical Equivalence Region

wide ranges of portfolios are statistically equivalent to the classical effi-cient frontier. Many portfolios are available based on the same informa-tion that produced classical efficiency that may be far more reasonable and practical investments. Indeed, it is unclear from the displays what reasonable portfolio might be excluded from the set of statistically equivalent efficient portfolios.[10] The results highlight the need for and importance of a statistical understanding of MV optimization.[11]

RANK-ASSOCIATED EFFICIENT PORTFOLIOS

While useful for understanding the ambiguity of MV optimality, Exhibit 5.2 does not identify which portfolios under the classical curve are associated with a given portfolio on the MV efficient frontier. For example, what stat-istically equivalent portfolios are associated with the minimum variance, a middle, or the maximum return portfolios on the efficient frontier?

Recall from the construction process that the minimum variance port-folio has rank 1 relative to the 51 efficient portfolios computed in each simulated efficient frontier; the maximum average return portfolio has rank 51 in each simulated efficient frontier. Therefore, any portfolio on the classical efficient frontier may be associated with similarly ranked port-folios on the different simulated efficient frontiers. For future reference,

10. In a related study, Chopra (1991) provides a simple three-asset example that illustrates how nearly optimal portfolios can be dramatically different in composition.
11. Statistical issues will be developed formally in Chapter 7.

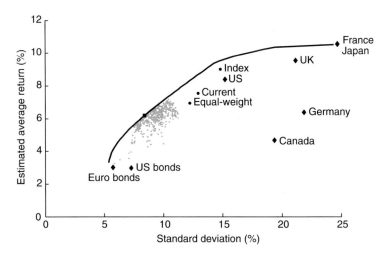

Exhibit 5.3 Middle Efficient Statistical Equivalent MV Portfolios

define the 21st efficient frontier portfolio in return rank as the "middle" efficient frontier portfolio in Exhibit 4.1.[12]

The associated minimum variance portfolios cluster nearly indistinguishably close to the minimum variance classical efficient portfolio so that they are nearly indistinguishable. The maximum return simulated portfolios consist of only the highest return assets, so they are easily associated. The middle associated MV optimal portfolios are the most interesting. Exhibit 5.3 displays the 500 rank-associated statistically equivalent MV efficient portfolios for the middle (21 rank) portfolio. A circle indicates the position of the middle portfolio on the efficient frontier. The exhibit shows that the rank-associated simulated portfolios represent a sparse area under the curve. The shape of the rank-associated regions varies in interesting ways depending on the position of the portfolio on the MV efficient frontier.

HOW PRACTICAL AN INVESTMENT TOOL?

The statistical character of linear constrained MV optimal portfolios in the context of estimation error has significant implications for investment practice. In particular, many investment organizations devote a great deal of time and effort to formulating and managing optimization inputs. The size of the statistical equivalence region in Exhibit 5.2 suggests that such

---

12. Subsequent discussions use this definition consistently. The ranking is from lowest to highest average return.

practices may have marginal investment value relative to addressing the impact of estimation error on defining portfolio optimality.[13]

Faced with the level of variability inherent in MV portfolio optimization, should an investor abandon the technology? This is, in fact, a very reasonable conclusion.[14] MV optimization typically misuses investment information. The ambiguity of traditional MV optimization as a result of estimation error opens the door to a fundamentally new statistical perception of MV efficiency. We develop a number of procedures statistically informed to enhance the practical value of MV optimized portfolios. These include:

1. Resampled Efficient Frontier™ optimization
2. Resampled Efficiency™ rebalancing, monitoring, analysis
3. Stein estimation
4. Bayesian estimation
5. Avoiding optimization design errors

Each of these procedures can help to improve the investment value of optimized portfolios. Together they can have a substantial impact on the value of the optimization process. Properly managed, the outlook for MV optimization as a practical tool of investment management should be cautious optimism.

---

13. We will have more to say on this subject later in our discussion of Markowitz and Usmen (2003) and Stein estimators in chapters 8 and 11.
14. See the comments in Jobson and Korkie (1981).

6

The Resampled Efficient Frontier™

This chapter introduces Resampled Efficient Frontier (REF) optimization, a generalization of linear constrained Markowitz MV portfolio optimization that includes uncertainty in investment information in the optimization process.[1] Monte Carlo resampling methods are used to more realistically condition investment information in the optimization. REF optimality avoids the literal use of investment information characteristic of classical MV and other portfolio optimization methods. Under practical assumptions, REF optimization is provably effective at improving linear constrained risk-adjusted portfolio return on average.[2] REF optimality typically leads to a more effective level of diversification and risk management than previously available. The resampling process also allows customization of the optimization process relative to investment mandates, objectives, strategies, and information character.

EFFICIENT FRONTIER STATISTICAL ANALYSIS

The enormous variation of Monte Carlo efficient frontier simulations in Exhibit 5.1 demonstrates the need for a statistical view of MV efficiency.

---

1. RE optimization was invented by Richard Michaud and Robert Michaud and is a U.S. patented procedure, worldwide patents pending. It was originally described in Michaud (1998, Chapter 6). New Frontier Advisors, LLC (NFA) is exclusive worldwide licensee.
2. This chapter addresses sign-constrained portfolio optimization, generally the framework of choice for institutional asset allocation. Index-relative and long-short optimization, often used in institutional equity portfolio management, is treated in Chapter 9.

In Exhibit 5.1, every simulated MV efficient frontier is the right way to invest for a given set of inputs. However, the inputs are highly uncertain: how should an investor use the portfolio optimality uncertainty displayed in the exhibit? From one perspective, the instability of MV efficiency with estimation error demonstrated in the exhibit may indicate little hope of practical investment value. In reality, the variation suggests a statistical route for transforming MV optimization into a more investment useful procedure.

For a highly risk-averse investor, the minimum variance portfolio is the optimal portfolio for any simulated efficient frontier. Since all simulated efficient frontiers are equally likely, Resampled Efficiency™ (RE) defines the optimal minimum variance portfolio as the average of the portfolio weights of all the simulated minimum variance portfolios. Exhibit 6.1 shows the optimal minimum variance portfolio plotted at the base of the lower, REF, curve in Exhibit 6.1.

For a risk-indifferent investor, the maximum return portfolio is the optimal portfolio for any given simulated efficient frontier. Since all simulated maximum return portfolios are equally likely, the RE optimal maximum return portfolio is defined as the average of the portfolio weights of all the simulated maximum return portfolios and is plotted at the top of the lower curve in Exhibit 6.1.

Similarly, RE optimality can be defined for the utility function that characterizes any investor's risk-return preferences. The average of the maximum expected utility tangent portfolios on simulated MV efficient

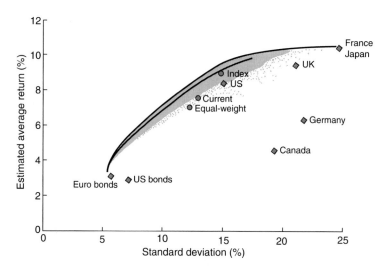

Exhibit 6.1 Mean-Variance and Resampled Efficient Frontiers

frontiers in Exhibit 5.1 defines the RE optimal portfolio. The REF plots as the lower curve in Exhibit 6.1 and is the collection of all possible RE optimal portfolios with risk aversion parameters from expected utility curves ranging from total risk aversion to total risk indifference.[3,4] The exhibit shows that the REF lies within the range of estimation error alternative optimal portfolios as shown in Exhibit 5.2. The results demonstrate that REF portfolios reflect safer, less extreme investments when uncertainty in investment information is considered. More generally, the REF is based on averages of all properly associated optimal portfolios on the simulated MV efficient frontiers.[5,6]

Table 6.1 displays the minimum variance, middle, and maximum average return portfolios from the two efficient frontiers in Exhibit 6.1. Little difference exists between RE and MV optimal portfolios at very low risk. Of course, this is a simple example consisting of only eight assets; larger optimization universes may find important differences. As indicated in columns 4 and 5 of Table 6.1, moderate-risk portfolios display more pronounced optimality differences; the RE portfolio is more diversified and has less extreme large and small allocations. Columns 6 and 7 in Table 6.1 display the dramatic difference between the maximum return MV and RE portfolios; the MV portfolio is a single asset while the RE portfolio is a an investment-intuitive, diversified portfolio.[7]

3. This construction process is consistent with λ-association as described in the appendix. The process highlights how rational agents may make investment decisions that lead to REF optimality. A concern (e.g., Markowitz & Usmen, 2003) that the REF is not consistent with rational agent decision making may be due to the original description of the procedure in the Michaud (1998) text that used rank-association, a heuristic construction process, seemingly devoid of utility considerations. Rank-order association is used as a convenient compute-efficient approximation to utility-based REF construction. Our views on rationality axioms and rule-based systems are discussed further in Michaud (2003, fn. 6).

4. The examples in the text use rank-order association for computing the REF portfolios. The illustrations are based on computing 51 portfolios equally spaced from low to high return for the classical and each simulated efficient frontier. The RE portfolio is computed as the average of the rank-associated simulated MV efficient portfolios. The REF portfolios are the collection of the RE portfolios associated with an MV efficient frontier. The procedure is a useful, simple, compute-efficient, and statistically stable estimate of utility-function-based REF portfolios. Other approximations are also available with various compute-efficiency and statistical stability characteristics.

5. Mathematically, REF optimality is an integral in portfolio space of the expected value of the MV optimal portfolio weights. The resampling/bootstrap process is a Monte Carlo method for spanning for a given level of uncertainty the linear-constraint-defined portfolio space probabilistically and estimating the integral.

6. It may be of interest to note a statistical perspective on the innovation implicit in the definition of the REF. Resampling and bootstrap methods in statistics are generally concerned with exploring the variability implicit in historical data, as in Efron (2005). RE optimization uses the variability exposed by resampling to define a new statistic that did not exist before.

7. In this case, there is a simple interpretation and analytical derivation of the RE maximum return optimal portfolio. Each asset weight is equal to the probability that it is truly the maximum return asset.

Table 6.1 RE and MV Minimum Variance, Middle, Maximum Return Portfolios

Assets	Min Variance		Middle		Max Return	
	RE	MV	RE	MV	RE	MV
Euro Bonds	98%	99%	37%	44%	0%	0%
US Bonds	0%	0%	9%	0%	0%	0%
Canada	0%	0%	1%	0%	1%	0%
France	0%	0%	8%	5%	34%	100%
Germany	0%	0%	3%	0%	4%	0%
Japan	2%	1%	13%	15%	33%	0%
UK	0%	0%	7%	3%	16%	0%
US	0%	0%	22%	32%	12%	0%

PROPERTIES OF RESAMPLED EFFICIENT FRONTIER PORTFOLIOS

As indicated by Exhibit 6.1, REF portfolios lie below and generally well within the range of portfolio risk spanned by the MV efficient frontier.[8] The REF is not a statistical artifact of portfolio simulation but represents a computable alternative set of investments. The question of interest is whether REF portfolios provide an investment-relevant and practical alternative for defining portfolio optimality.

From a superficial point of view, RE optimization appears to be an inferior investment framework. This is because the REF expects less return and has a more restricted range of risk relative to classical efficiency. In-sample studies of portfolio efficiency, such as Harvey et al. (2003), conclude that the REF does not define optimal portfolios.[9] The apparent inferiority of REF portfolios provides the first glimpse, one of many, of the limitations of in-sample MV efficiency portfolio analysis.[10]

The appropriate interpretation of REF versus classical MV optimality is straightforward. If you are 100% certain of your risk-return estimates (to 16 decimal places of accuracy or more), the Markowitz efficient frontier is the appropriate definition of portfolio efficiency.[11] If you are less than 100% certain of your risk-return estimates, you expect less return and are less willing to put money at risk, and REF optimality is appropriate. The REF properly reflects portfolio optimization in the context of

---

8. In some cases the REF may extend beyond the MV efficient frontier. These cases are not material to our discussion here.

9. In-sample utility is greater for classical than REF portfolios. As discussed below, the Harvey et al. (2003) investor is unlikely to be pleased with their "more optimal" solution.

10. One of the most important contributions of REF analysis is the notion that in-sample MV efficiency analysis is an unreliable and often misleading framework for portfolio analysis. Implications for asset management are discussed specifically in Michaud and Michaud (2005b) and later in the text.

11. As noted in Chapter 4, computed MV efficient frontier portfolios reflect 16 decimal places of accuracy for most modern computers.

information uncertainty. To drive the point home, consider an investor with a complete lack of certainty in his or her investment information. In this case the optimal efficient frontier is the no-information prior portfolio, either equal or benchmark weighted.[12] The REF portfolio is the no-information portfolio in this case, while Markowitz optimization remains insensitive to information uncertainty.[13] RE optimization is the paradigm of choice for rational decision making under conditions of information uncertainty.

As Exhibit 6.1 illustrates, the RE and MV frontiers may be close in MV space. A superficial reading may suggest that the procedures produce similar solutions. Exhibit 6.2 is a portfolio composition map of the MV and RE optimal asset allocations in Exhibit 6.1. Each band of shading represents one of the eight assets in the base case. A vertical strip through the bands provides the optimal portfolio allocations at that risk level. The portfolios with minimum variance appear on the left-hand side of the charts, high-return portfolios on the right. The upper panel presents the composition map for MV efficiency; the lower panel depicts RE optimality. In the left-hand side of each panel, the dark area represents nearly a 100% allocation to Euro bonds at the low-risk end of the efficient frontiers.

Exhibit 6.2 shows that the MV efficient frontier includes only five out of the eight assets: Euro bonds and U.S., U.K., Japanese, and French equities. If the return estimate for U.K. equities (middle asset in the MV map) is reduced by 0.5%, the allocation to U.K. equities disappears across the entire classical frontier. Since the standard error of the expected return for the U.K. equities is much larger than 0.5%, this result reflects far more sensitivity than is desirable or sensible for a statistically insignificant change. Similar, or more extreme, examples of statistical insensitivity and instability can be found on nearly every MV frontier.

The composition map for the REF illustrates very different properties. REF optimality includes all eight assets. The allocations transition smoothly from one risk level to another. A reduced estimate of return for U.K. equities by 0.5% produces a hardly noticeable change in optimal allocations across the entire frontier. RE optimization is robust and fundamentally different in character and allocations, even when the two frontiers are similar in in-sample MV space.[14]

---

12. It is a necessary condition that the risk spectrum for estimation error-sensitive MV portfolio efficiency converges to the no-information portfolio as uncertainty increases. This property contradicts the properties of the heuristic Feldman (2003) and Ceria and Stubbs (2005) methods, where the risk spectrum is constant and equal to classical efficiency whatever the level of certainty in investment information. It also contradicts the conclusions of the Chopra and Ziemba (1993) study. Our results demonstrate that estimation error in risk as well as return is necessary for appropriately defining portfolio optimality under information uncertainty.
13. Changing the level of forecast certainty in the RE optimization process is discussed further below.
14. Ad hoc portfolio constraints are often put in place to improve the stability of the MV optimized solution. Ironically, they can often introduce instability rather than reduce it. Consider the following

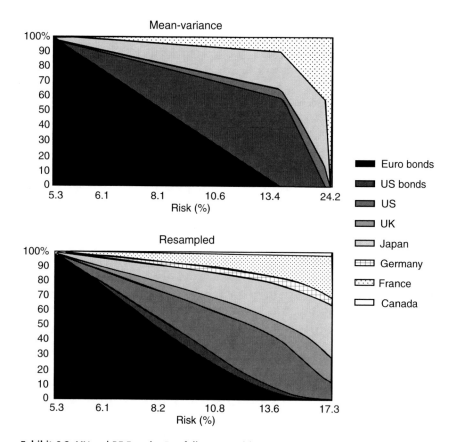

Exhibit 6.2 MV and RE Frontier Portfolio Composition Maps

TRUE AND ESTIMATED OPTIMIZATION INPUTS

Markowitz gives you the right way to invest given that you happen to know that your risk-return estimates are correct. Under these conditions, no other set of input assumptions or set of portfolios is more appropriate as a basis for investment. Although the Markowitz MV efficient frontier portfolios are not necessarily the investment performance winners for a given draw of returns in the investment period, on average they are the

example: in an optimization of many assets, two assets (assets A and B) have similar risk and return characteristics. Suppose the optimizer weights assets A and B in similar proportion along the unconstrained frontier. If a binding upper bound were introduced for asset B, asset A would increase at a greater rate along the frontier to make up for the unavailable asset B. Similarly, if asset B is constrained but the forecast returns vary for asset A, the volatility of the optimal portfolio weight of asset A would be increased. Improperly implemented, constraints can form a knife-edge, forcing the optimizer to make sharp decisions and leading to greater portfolio weight instability. The RE optimization creates robust solutions by averaging all the knife-edge MV optimizations relative to the uncertainty in the information.

best-performing for a given risk level for perfect certainty.[15] In this case, REF optimality has little investment interest.

The problem with the scenario in the previous paragraph, and its conclusion, is that it is completely unrealistic. The true value of optimization inputs is unknown and unknowable. Risk-return estimates in practice include substantial estimation error and are at best an informed guess of the true values in the investment period. As demonstrated in Exhibits 5.1 and 5.2, what characterizes MV portfolio optimization is its extreme sensitivity to estimation errors.[16] RE optimization addresses the issue of estimation error sensitivity intrinsic to MV efficiency.

One of the most attractive features of REF portfolios in practice is that they are often consistent with investment intuition without the need for ad hoc constraints. For example, the maximum return MV efficient portfolio in Exhibit 6.1 represents a 100% bet on French equities. However, the optimization inputs for Japanese and French equities in Table 2.3 are virtually identical. Based purely on these inputs, investors are likely to prefer an equal bet on both markets. In addition, from a return/risk basis, the inputs for U.K. and U.S. equities are not very different from Japanese and French equities. Consequently, the diverse RE efficient portfolio is preferable to the MV efficient 100% bet on French equities. The reduced range of risk simply reflects the need for more diverse optimal portfolios and is a direct consequence of the uncertainty in investment information ignored in classical efficiency.[17]

RE portfolios depend less on any particular characteristic of the optimization inputs. They reflect less extreme portfolio weights than MV portfolios. Because REF portfolios are averages, not outliers, they are more likely to provide safe and reliable investments with better out-of-sample performance on average. Note that REF portfolios with more moderate bets on assets may have additional practical investment benefits, from reduced liquidity demands to lower trading costs in portfolio rebalancings.

SIMULATION PROOFS OF RESAMPLED EFFICIENCY OPTIMIZATION

RE optimized portfolios have many desirable investment properties. However, as we will show, one of the most important features of RE optimization is its provable performance superiority on average under

---

15. This point is just statistics. In any random draw of investment returns, there is a likelihood that actual events deviate from underlying population statistical parameters in the same way that tossing a fair coin 10 times will not always result in five heads.

16. Simulation studies implicitly assume that the return distribution reflected in the historic data is stationary for the investment horizon of interest. The non-stationarity of the return distribution adds another significant dimension of estimation error to portfolio optimization in practice.

17. Note that even in a two-asset optimization, REF optimality provides useful information by limiting risk taking at the high end of the frontier.

practical investment assumptions.[18] Jobson and Korkie (1981) tested the investment performance of unbounded versus equal-weighted portfolios using simulation proofs. Their procedure can be used to test the investment performance of MV versus RE linearly constrained optimized portfolios.[19]

In a simulation study, the referee is assumed to know the true set of risk-returns for the assets. For this simulation study, the base case data (Tables 2.3 and 2.4) represent the true risk-returns.[20] The referee does not tell investors the true values but provides a set of Monte Carlo simulated returns consistent with the true risks and returns.[21] In the base case data set, each simulation consists of 18 years of monthly returns and represents a possible out-of-sample realization of the true values of the optimization parameters. Each set of simulated returns results in an estimate (with estimation error) of the optimization parameters and an MV efficient frontier. Each MV efficient frontier and set of estimated optimization parameters defines an RE optimized frontier. This process is repeated many times.[22] In each of the simulations of MV and RE optimized frontiers, the referee uses the true risk-return values to score the actual risks and returns of the optimized portfolios.

The averaged results of the simulation study are displayed in Exhibit 6.3. The upper dotted curves display the in-sample averaged MV and RE frontiers that were submitted to the referee for scoring. The higher dotted curve is the MV efficient frontier; the lower dotted curve is the REF. The portfolios are plotted based on the simulated risks and returns. However, the referee knows the true risks and returns for each simulated optimized portfolio. The bottom solid curves in Exhibit 6.3 display the average of the true, out-of-sample, risks and returns of the optimized portfolios. The higher solid curve represents the RE optimized results, the lower solid curve the Markowitz optimized results. The lower curves in the exhibit show that the RE optimized portfolios, on average, achieve roughly the

---

18. A simulation proof requires assumptions about the true distribution of assets. The "truth" data set has to be in good financial order for the simulation to properly represent a useful out-of-sample investment process. Historical data may not always reflect a financially relevant truth data set because it may often include dominated assets. For example, the monthly returns for the default data set of indices for the 10-year period from January 1996 to December 2005 exhibits a negative average return for the Japanese index. In this case Japan is a dominated asset relative to other assets in the optimization universe and investment in Japan in the context of sign constraints makes no sense. Dominated assets that are inconsistent with a relevant financial "truth" in the context of sign constraints for simulation study purposes need to be excluded. While RE optimization can't be proven to have higher out-of-sample risk-return in all possible simulation tests, properly implemented it outperforms for financially relevant cases of practical interest. Appendix B provides a geometric proof of superiority that is data-set-independent. The tests in this chapter assume sign-constrained optimization. The tests in Chapter 9 treat the index-relative and associated long-short case.

19. Simulation tests are preferable relative to back tests since back tests are time period dependent and there are not enough observations available to test for statistical significance.

20. We are indebted to Olivier Ledoit for critical assistance in defining the test framework.

21. Our simulations assume multivariate normal returns.

22. A minimum of 500 simulations of the MV and RE frontiers is used in the study.

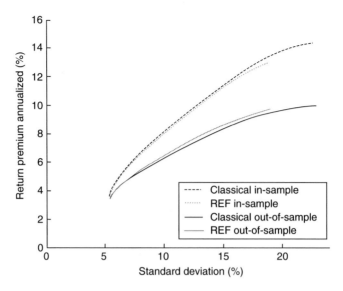

Exhibit 6.3 MV and RE Optimized Portfolio Out-of-Sample Performance

same return with less risk, or alternatively more return with the same level of risk, relative to the Markowitz portfolios.[23] The results represent the average out-of-sample investment experience of an investor using either MV or RE portfolios.

The simulation experiment illustrates that the RE optimized portfolios are, on average, provably effective at improving risk-adjusted investment performance.[24] RE optimized portfolios perform better because they are better risk-managed by avoiding the unrealistically literal use of investment information that characterizes Markowitz MV optimization.[25]

It should be noted that the simulation results presented are very conservative. In practice estimation error is far more prevalent than that represented by a stationary distribution of simulated monthly returns over an 18-year investment period. Reducing the number of simulated

23. Markowitz and Usmen (2003) replicated the results with the same data set.
24. Some notes need to accompany the proofs of enhanced investment value in Exhibit 6.3. The results assume total or real return, sign and budget constrained, MV optimized portfolios. The conclusions are generalizable for the leverage constraints typically imposed in practice. Leverage simply extends the frontiers. The index- or benchmark-relative case and associated long-short issues are discussed in Chapter 9. Note that because Euro bonds effectively dominate U.S. bonds on a risk-return basis, classical efficiency outperforms REF portfolios at extremely low risk. In this case, there is little ambiguity associated with the optimal minimum variance portfolio for this data set. In practice, however, Euro bond estimation error is unknown and an investor would be unable to rely on low-risk dominance in the investment period. This is an additional though more subtle example of the impact of including dominated assets in simulation studies.
25. Knight and Satchell (2006) find no benefit to RE optimization. However, they examine only the unbounded asset weight case as in Chapter 4.

returns increases estimation error to more realistic levels and enhances the relative benefits associated with RE optimized portfolios. More importantly, return distributions are not stationary in investment practice. The many scenarios simulated from investment information engineer a portfolio optimality designed to protect investments from unlikely perverse events.

WHY DOES IT WORK

In institutional asset allocation practice, optimization universes consist of investment-attractive assets.[26] As Merton (1987) observes, the optimization universe should consist of what you know. Nonnegative sign constraints are consistent with an all-assets-investable prior.[27] Frost and Savarino (1988) demonstrate that out-of-sample MV optimized portfolio performance may be enhanced by combining sign constraints with resampling data. An equally weighted portfolio is a candidate optimal allocation in this context.

Sign constraints impose valuable investment structure on each resampled MV efficient frontier. They act as Bayesian priors to create a bias in the structure of the resampled optimized portfolios, using the uncertainty of the resampling process to define candidate optimal portfolios. By definition, the average of the resampled MV efficient portfolios is not an outlier but reflects the uncertainty inherent in investment information.[28] The simulations show that the averaging process leads to improved average out-of-sample performance.[29]

CERTAINTY LEVEL AND RE OPTIMALITY

Up until now, each simulated MV efficient frontier discussed has been computed by simulating 18 years of monthly returns relative to the data in tables 2.3 and 2.4. The reason for simulating 18 years of monthly returns is to be consistent with the information level in the original data set. However, in general, investors do not know that their risk-return estimates reflect a specific level of information.

The number of simulated returns used to compute the simulated MV efficient frontiers is a free parameter of the RE optimization process. As the number of returns becomes large, the set of simulated risk-return

26. Lottery tickets and postage stamps are asset classes typically ignored in an institutional asset allocation.

27. Including leverage requires a trivial change in the argument and does not invalidate our conclusions.

28. Moderation of extreme portfolio weights is a characteristic of Stein estimators, discussed in Chapter 8. Bayes estimation, discussed in Chapter 11, may also moderate extreme portfolio weights. In contrast to RE optimization, these alternatives operate by changing the inputs prior to initiating the optimization process

29. Appendix B provides a geometric perception for understanding why RE optimization works.

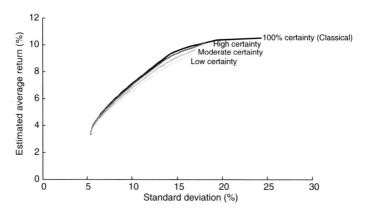

Exhibit 6.4 MV and REF Forecast Confidence Levels

estimates approaches the original risk-return estimates and the REF approaches the MV efficient frontier. When the number of observations becomes small, the REF approaches the no-information prior efficient port-folio. The number of simulated returns is a natural parameter for model-ing the confidence an investor has in risk-return estimates. Exhibit 6.4 illustrates RE optimal frontiers at different Forecast Confidence™ (FC) levels.[30,31] As the level of certainty increases, the REF approaches classical MV efficiency. The notion of FC level leads to a fundamental insight: RE optimization is simply a generalization of Markowitz MV optimization that allows investors to control the amount of confidence they have in their investment information in the optimization process.

FC LEVEL APPLICATIONS

One of the most serious critiques of classical portfolio optimization is asset management rigidity. The market outlook is an important consid-eration for many investment managers. Different style managers use investment information very differently and often reflect very different views and valuations of similar assets. Yet classical optimization is indif-ferent to the character and source of investment information. Classical investment process rigidity is a key reason for the indifference or lack of confidence many institutional managers exhibit toward portfolio optimi-zation technology.

In contrast, RE optimization is a flexible framework for portfolio opti-mization in asset management. In particular, the FC level is a valuable

---

30. Forecast Confidence level is a patent-pending procedure.
31. To facilitate the user experience, the Forecast Confidence (FC) level scale ranges from 1 to 10, indicating very low to very high information level. On this scale Markowitz optimization is an 11 and complete uncertainty 0. See further discussion and applications in Michaud and Michaud (2004a).

tool for customizing RE optimization to a manager's investment process. For example, variation in the FC level in the optimization may be used to reflect changes in confidence in the market outlook. Growth stock managers may wish to raise FC levels to reduce portfolio diversification, reflecting the more ephemeral near-term character of their information, while value managers may wish to lower FC levels to increase diversification, reflecting the longer-term character of their information. The ability to customize as well as create optimized investment strategies is a hallmark of the RE optimization process.

THE REF MAXIMUM RETURN POINT (MRP)

The statistical nature of RE portfolio optimization leads to some significant differences from classical MV optimization. For instance, the REF frontier may peak and then curve downward.[32] This turning point is the "maximum return point" (MRP) of the REF. The possible existence of an MRP is a key concept for understanding and using REF optimality.

Exhibit 6.5 illustrates how the REF MRP may arise. In each panel there are three high-risk assets; uncertainty is indicated by the ellipse around each point. The left-hand panel presumes an MV optimization level of certainty in information; the risk-returns are point estimates. The efficient frontier MRP portfolio includes only one asset. As uncertainty increases, as in the middle panel, there is less certainty concerning the return of the highest-return/risk asset; the REF includes some allocation to all three assets and the MRP REF portfolio lies below and to the left of the Markowitz maximum return portfolio. In the right-hand panel there is little certainty in the return of the highest-risk assets and the REF includes significant allocations in all three assets. In this case the MRP portfolio may emerge where the REF has a downward-sloping inefficient

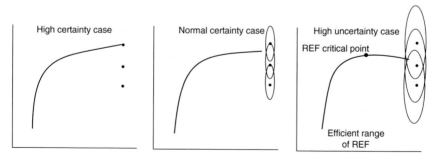

Exhibit 6.5 Forecast Certainty Levels and the REF Maximum Return Point

32. See Michaud and Michaud (2004b).

segment. Any risk beyond the MRP is not optimal and not on the REF by definition.

The REF MRP assures investors that the efficient maximum return portfolio is appropriately diversified. The MRP arises because RE optimization uses information from all assets in the optimization universe.[33] In contrast, since there is no notion of risk-return estimation uncertainty in classical MV optimization, investors may think that taking increasing amounts of risk is always justifiable.[34]

An REF MRP is relatively rare in institutional asset allocation studies. This is because assets in the optimization universe often have relatively similar attractive risk-return characteristics. In contrast, an REF MRP is often observed in large stock universe equity portfolio optimizations. This is because the optimization universe may have many assets that have relatively little return but much risk. The existence of high-risk assets with little return implies that high risk return is uncertain. As uncertainty increases, the uncertainty at high-risk portfolio levels reduces expected return and the REF exhibits an MRP. The identification of the REF MRP point prevents the overuse of inferior investments.[35] A necessary condition for a well-defined equity optimizer is to estimate the maximum level of risk that is consistent with the level of information in the optimization universe.[36]

There is an important associated issue in this context. Why would investors include statistically insignificant assets in the optimization universe? Merton (1987) teaches that the optimization universe should be defined in terms of investable assets. An optimizer is not capable of telling which investments are not investable; that is the role of the analyst. Including non-investable assets in an optimization is much like including bad information in a Bayesian prior. However, Merton's advice in the context of an equity optimization for a large stock index may result in unacceptably large tracking error risk and underrepresented sectors and industries. One simple solution is described in Michaud and Michaud (2005a): include an index-weighted composite asset of the statistically insignificant stocks in the index in the optimization.[37] The Merton principle of investing only in what you know remains the appropriate one.

---

33. Preliminary simulation tests are consistent with out-of-sample replication of in-sample REF MRPs.
34. The existence of the MRP is a useful way of justifying much institutional investment practice where assumed tracking error is often far less than the maximum available in a MV optimization. While active asset managers are sometimes critiqued for being closet indexers, a low level of active risk may only reflect a rational view of level of information in their estimates. Alternatively, not knowing the limits of efficient risk in an optimized portfolio may afflict asset management for many leveraged hedge fund managers.
35. Generally, low-return, high-risk securities have very small allocations in REF portfolios. More important is the financial rationale associated with their inclusion in the optimization.
36. The concept of the MRP has important applications in scaling returns and proper optimization design.
37. Further description and implications of using the composite asset are given in the reference and in Chapter 9.

IMPLICATIONS FOR ASSET MANAGEMENT

The REF plots below the classical frontier because it reflects uncertainty in investment information. As a consequence, the REF challenges much conventional academic and professional wisdom on optimality and management practice.

The REF challenges the results of many studies of in-sample utility function optimization of portfolios on the MV efficient frontier. Because REF portfolios have less estimated return and risk, in-sample utility studies find REF portfolios "less than optimal." But investors are very unlikely to prefer the "more optimal" portfolios on the MV efficient frontier if they promise less likely risk-adjusted return ex post. The consequence of ignoring out-of-sample performance of optimized portfolios is that many conclusions of in-sample utility studies are likely to be misleading or invalid.[38] Journal editors are well advised to require simulation studies of out-of-sample optimized portfolio performance in the context of estimation error as a matter of good practice.

The REF challenges the results of many studies based on analytical formulas derived from optimizing the in-sample information ratio (IR) or reward-to-risk ratio of portfolios on the unconstrained MV efficient frontier. In these studies the IR is used as an investment intuitive and practical surrogate for in-sample utility. In-sample studies for maximizing IR without estimation error lead to seductive though erroneous prescriptions for asset management, such as increasing the size of the optimization universe and trading frequently. While the analytic formulas for in-sample IR are improved, the out-of-sample consequences on performance of the optimized portfolios are ignored.[39] Not only are the prescriptions likely to be invalid, they are often the inverse of good investment practice.[40] Clearly, only a framework that ignores estimation error and out-of-sample performance could conclude that increasingly frequent trading would improve optimality.[41] Our studies demonstrate that considering the implications of estimation error on out-of-sample performance is essential for defining portfolio optimality and avoiding serious investment practice errors.[42]

CONCLUSION

RE is an important new tool for defining portfolio efficiency in practice. It is useful for understanding the statistical characteristics and

---

38. Examples include Harvey et al. (2003), who do not address out-of-sample performance of their "more optimal" utility functions, and Chopra and Ziemba (1993), who invalidly conclude that estimation error in risk can be ignored.
39. Examples include Grinold (1989), Grinold and Kahn (1994, Chapter 6), and Clarke et al. (2002, 2006).
40. More discussion is given in Michaud and Michaud (2005b).
41. Trading issues are discussed further in Chapter 7.
42. The composite asset procedure of Chapter 9 and other considerations for dealing with statistically insignificant investment information often reverses the prescriptions of IR based analytic formula studies.

practical limitations of MV efficiency. In addition, in the context of a relevant constraint prior, it is provably effective on average at enhancing the out-of-sample investment value of optimized portfolios. Relative to MV efficiency, resampled efficient portfolios are also likely to be more robust and investment intuitive, two useful characteristics in many institutional contexts.

APPENDIX A: RANK-VERSUS λ-ASSOCIATED RE PORTFOLIOS

Rank association is used in the text for computing RE optimal portfolios. One simple alternative is to associate simulated MV efficient frontier portfolios using a quadratic utility function. Given a value of λ (lambda), associate the efficient and simulated efficient linear constrained portfolios that minimize:

$$\phi = \sigma^2 - \lambda*\mu. \tag{6.1}$$

Each value of λ defines a specific portfolio on the MV and simulated efficient frontiers. Varying λ from zero to infinity spans the set of efficient and simulated efficient frontier portfolios. Table 6A.1 displays the true reward-to-risk ratios for MV and resampled efficiency in the same test procedure as in Exhibit 6.3, where λ is used to associate simulated with efficient portfolios. The λ values are shown in the first row of Tables 6A.1 and 6A.2.[43] λ- association appears to be slightly less statistically stable than rank-association. While rank-association is not always the procedure of choice, it is often a practical compromise.

Table 6A.1 Lambda-Associated True Reward-to-Risk Ratios, MV Efficiency

λ	0	10	15	20	50	100	infinity
Mean	0.178	0.201	0.200	0.195	0.170	0.152	0.127
Return (%)	3.3	4.4	5.0	5.5	8.1	9.3	9.9
Risk (%)	5.4	6.3	7.2	8.3	14.0	18.0	22.7

Table 6A.2 Lambda-Associated True Reward-to-Risk Ratios, Resampled Efficiency

λ	0	10	15	20	50	100	infinity
Mean	0.180	0.202	0.200	0.196	0.173	0.161	0.151
Return (%)	3.4	4.5	5.1	5.8	8.1	9.0	9.6
Risk (%)	5.4	6.4	7.4	8.6	13.6	16.3	18.5

43. For example, when λ equals 10, 15, and 20 in Table 6A.2, the average true risk is larger for resampled than for MV efficiency.

APPENDIX B: ROBERT'S HEDGEHOG

The following example helps to illustrate RE optimization.

Robert has a favorite pet hedgehog named Ralph. Ralph escaped from his cage and is now somewhere in the tall grass surrounding the house. Fortunately, Robert fitted Ralph with a GPS locator device, and the house is surrounded by a sturdy hedgehog-proof fence that Ralph can't burrow underneath. Therefore we can safely assume that Ralph is somewhere inside the fence, and we know that his GPS locator can pinpoint Ralph's location within a 10-meter radius circle. To find the hedgehog as quickly as possible, though, Robert wants to start his search where Ralph is most likely to be. How does Robert find his hedgehog?

Referring to Exhibit 6.6, we see that the GPS locator shows Ralph is somewhere in the circle with center A. Point A is therefore a place to start Robert's search. However Robert notes that A is outside of the fenced yard. So Robert narrows his search to the area indicated by the GPS system but within the fence. Points on the fence and within the circle close to point A are better starting points. Point M is the closest fenced point to A and is a more optimal place for Robert to begin his search for Ralph.[44]

Suppose the information used by the GPS locator system is statistically estimated and has estimation error. In this case it is useful to

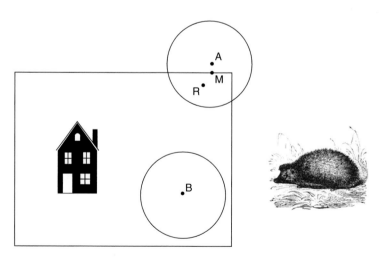

Exhibit 6.6 Robert's Yard

---

44. Hedgehog picture courtesy of Florida Center for Instructional Technology.

repeatedly query the GPS system and request new resampled estimates of the hedgehog's position that may vary materially with each estimate. Some of the resampled estimates similar to M may place Ralph at points along the fence; others would be in the yard's interior. Since there is no reason to choose one of the estimates over the others, we take an average of all solutions on the fence and in the yard. The resampled estimate of Ralph's location is likely to be near but not at the fence, as in point R. The resampled estimate is therefore likely to be a more realistic estimate of the actual position of Robert's hedgehog.

Our story has important implications for estimation of optimized portfolios. Suppose Ralph represents not a hedgehog in a two-dimensional yard but an optimal portfolio in high-dimensional portfolio space, and the signal comes not from a GPS but from an estimate of the return distribution of all assets. Point A, outside the fence, represents an unconstrained MV optimization estimate. Point M, at the fence, represents a Markowitz constrained MV optimization solution. Resampling the constrained MV problem gives multiple solutions along the boundary and interior of the solution space. Point R, the average of these solutions, represents the RE optimization solution. R is a better, more realistic solution than M because it includes all the information associated with Markowitz optimization as well as addressing estimation error.

Of course, finding Ralph is a lot simpler than finding an optimal portfolio. We know things exactly in Ralph's case that we can only estimate for a real problem. For example, we know exactly what the boundary and confidence region look like for Ralph but must estimate those for the portfolio problem. Another fundamental difference is the complexity of the problem. Finding Ralph is a linear problem: if the GPS is off by a meter, Robert's search will be off by about a meter. Finding an optimal portfolio requires inversion of the covariance matrix (among other things), which is not linear at all.[45] In the base case data, this complexity translates to an error multiplier of up to 528.

Note the circle centered at point B. It is natural to ask what happens when there is no fence or the GPS estimate is wholly within the yard as in B. In these cases, the Markowitz and RE optimizations do not improve the estimate. However, linear constraints are always present in practice. Moreover, as Jobson and Korkie have shown, the instability of unconstrained MV optimization in the presence of estimation error implies that B is a very poor estimate of true MV optimality.

Our story demonstrates that, properly used, RE optimization is a never worse, more stable, and likely more realistic solution for computing

---

45. The error associated with this process relates to the condition number of the covariance matrix. The condition number is a measure of how close to singular the covariance matrix is. Inverting a nearly singular covariance matrix is analogous to dividing by a number close to zero.

MV optimized portfolios in practical investment contexts.[46] Because MV optimization is very sensitive to estimation error, the benefits of RE relative to MV optimization are likely to be highly investment significant. It has not escaped our notice that the results do not depend on a quadratic objective. They may apply to any maximization or optimization problem with estimation error in the context of informative constraints.

---

46. Estimation error always exists in practice. As Chapter 9 will indicate, an index-relative or long-short optimization framework may require a different approach for defining constraints than the traditional asset allocations in this chapter.

7

Portfolio Rebalancing, Analysis, and Monitoring

Investment information is often statistically insignificant.[1] MV optimization is insensitive to investment insignificance, resulting in frequent but ineffective and costly portfolio rebalancings. In current investment practice, portfolio rebalancing and monitoring rules are largely ad hoc. For example, institutions commonly rebalance their portfolios on a calendar basis, such as monthly, quarterly, or annually. Another widely used rule is to rebalance a portfolio if asset weights exceed a predetermined fixed range, such as ±5%, of optimal or benchmark weights. Ad hoc rules exist to limit the number of rebalancings and to avoid trading on insignificant information.

A proper and reliable portfolio rebalancing rule is necessarily statistical. An investor will want to know whether trading a portfolio for a presumably more optimal one is likely to significantly improve performance in the investment period. If the current portfolio is not statistically significantly different from the optimal, trading is unlikely to be productive. The challenge lies in identifying statistically significant differences.

This chapter introduces statistically based rigorous portfolio trading rules for linear constrained MV optimized portfolios. Rigorous statistical rules have not been available until now because standard analytical techniques do not treat linear constrained MV optimization.[2] Rebalancing rules for linearly constrained MV optimized portfolios require properly

---

1. This fact is particularly the case in large index equity portfolio optimization.
2. See Shanken (1985) for a statistical test in the context of unbounded MV optimization.

applied resampling and bootstrapping techniques. Our new patented procedures will also be useful for portfolio monitoring and asset importance analyses.[3]

RESAMPLED EFFICIENCY AND DISTANCE FUNCTIONS

Optimization information is always uncertain in practice; consequently, in this chapter, RE optimality defines the notion of portfolio efficiency.[4] An RE optimal portfolio is an average of properly associated efficient frontier portfolios. In statistical parlance, the portfolio weights of an RE optimal portfolio represent a sample mean vector. The statistical properties of a sample mean vector are mathematically and statistically convenient.

From a statistical perspective, a portfolio is efficient with respect to a desired REF optimal portfolio if the portfolio weight vectors differ insignificantly. A "distance" function measures the difference between the portfolio weights. Distance functions identify the possible significance of the need-to-trade probability and therefore when trading is, or is not, needed for improved investment performance.

Many pitfalls accompany the search for a financially relevant distance function for portfolio statistical analysis. REF optimal portfolios represent linear constrained sample mean vectors. In the unconstrained case of Chapter 4, resampled portfolio weights have a well-known probability distribution.[5] With unconstrained portfolios, inference with respect to statistical differences between resampled optimal and candidate portfolio weights is straightforward.[6] Statistical inference is associated with a test statistic that operates as a multi-asset distance function. Unfortunately, linear constrained REF portfolios invalidate the statistical assumptions of standard procedures. One of the principal goals of resampling and bootstrap methods is to define test statistics and confidence sets in situations where standard statistical methods may not be available or yield exact answers. Resampling is the method of choice for developing valid statistically rigorous portfolio rebalancing rules for linear constrained MV optimized portfolios.

Since standard statistical tests for linear constrained MV optimized portfolios are unavailable, a distance function in the context of a resampling process provides a useful alternative. Unfortunately, there are a number of financially invalid approaches for defining a distance function.

---

3. The RE rebalancing procedures in this chapter were invented by Robert Michaud and Richard Michaud and are protected by U.S. patents. New Frontier Advisors, LLC is worldwide licensee.

4. The procedures in this chapter apply to sign-constrained as well as index-relative or long-short portfolios.

5. The usual assumptions include multivariate normal returns or sufficiently large random samples.

6. Hotellings' T^2 is often the basis of such a procedure. See the appendix for further description of confidence regions and inference for the sample mean vector under standard assumptions.

An obvious but invalid proposal is to use a Euclidean metric (square root of the sum of squared differences between corresponding weights of the two portfolios) for defining the distance between two portfolios. A financially valid portfolio distance metric requires consideration of portfolio risk in aggregate, including correlations.[7]

The relative variance is a financially useful metric for defining the distance between two portfolios. Formula (7.1) defines the relative variance between portfolio P, the current portfolio, and P_0, the RE optimal portfolio.[8] Σ is the covariance matrix used in the optimization. For illustrative purposes, see the data in Tables 2.3 and 2.4. Formula (7.1) is the basis of the RE rebalancing studies in the remainder of the chapter.

$$(P - P_0)'*\Sigma*(P - P_0) \tag{7.1}$$

PORTFOLIO NEED-TO-TRADE PROBABILITY

The resampling process provides a simple means of computing a probability distribution based on the test statistic in formula (7.1). We proceed as follows.

Compute simulated MV efficient frontiers and the associated optimal portfolios for a given REF portfolio P_0.[9] Sort the distances or relative variances according to formula (7.1) from small to large. Compute the percentile value of the sorted relative variances according to a given need-to-trade probability; for example, a 90% need-to-trade probability is a portfolio relative variance equal to the 90th percentile value of the sorted relative variances. The 90th percentile represents the fact that 90% of the relative variances of simulated optimal portfolios are as close as or closer to REF optimal. Any portfolio with a relative variance greater than the 90th percentile value is said to have (at least) a 90% need-to-trade probability. A 90% need-to-trade probability may often indicate that rebalancing is recommended. In contrast, a 10% need-to-trade probability may often indicate little reason to trade.

It should be noted that the trading implications of a need-to-trade probability depend greatly on the manager's investment strategy, available data, investment horizon, and outlook. A value manager often sets a higher-threshold need-to-trade probability than a growth stock or momentum or statistical arbitrage manager. Note that the need-to-trade probability is a portfolio-based rebalancing rule. The distribution of the relative variances varies with the REF portfolio.

7. More than one kind of distance or metric function can and may be used. The one we choose for illustration is generally the most easily understood and widely relevant for investment practice.

8. Formula 7.1 assumes vector and matrix operations. The term $(P-P_0)$ is the difference vector of portfolio weights. The term $(P-P_0)'$ is the transpose of the difference vector. Σ is the return covariance matrix. The result of the matrix and vector products is a number.

9. One approach for defining association is the rank-association procedure described in Chapters 5 and 6. Other association procedures are discussed later in this chapter.

The limitations of the above procedure, originally described in Michaud (1998, Chapter 7), can be seen most vividly when considering the REF maximum return portfolio. To illustrate, consider the base case data. Each associated simulated MV efficient portfolio relative to the maximum REF portfolio consists of a single asset; in other words, each simulated maximum return efficient portfolio is 100% in France, Japan, and so forth. While the REF maximum return optimal portfolio is well diversified, none of the associated simulated MV efficient portfolios that would be used in the definition of relative variances are REF diversified. The fact that the associated portfolios are not RE optimal diversified portfolios limited the power of the original statistical test. The problem is that the associated portfolios are not RE optimal diversified portfolios. This is the problem solved by the meta-resampling process described below.

META-RESAMPLING PORTFOLIO REBALANCING

The objective of the meta-resampling procedure is to properly associate simulated RE optimal portfolios with REF optimal portfolios in the portfolio rebalancing rule.

The meta-resampling procedure repeats the steps required for computing REF optimal portfolios but adds an additional step: compute an REF for each simulated MV efficient frontier computed in the original process. One way of describing the new procedure is that each simulated "parent" MV efficient frontier spawns a "child" REF. The association process in formula (7.1) replaces parent MV efficient frontier portfolios with child REF simulated portfolios. Returning to the maximum return REF portfolio, the relative variances in formula (7.1) are computed with the maximum return child RE optimal portfolio. All portfolios in the meta-resampled need-to-trade probability estimation procedure are RE optimal portfolios. Exhibit 7.1 provides an illustration of the set of meta-resampled optimized portfolios associated with the middle REF portfolio and can be compared to Exhibit 5.3 without meta-resampling. Unlike Exhibit 5.3, the associated meta-resampled portfolios are nicely compact around the REF portfolio.

Meta-resampling does not change the definition of REF optimality;[10] meta-resampling simply changes the statistical characteristics of the associated portfolios for the need-to-trade probability rule. The statistical power of the meta-resampled need-to-trade probability rule is fairly uniform across the entire frontier. This fact is a significant enhancement of the original procedure. The meta-resampling process also corrects the statistical limitations that existed in the applications of the need-to-trade rule. For example, the enhanced procedure markedly reduces the skewness of asset

---

10. An average of averages is still the average.

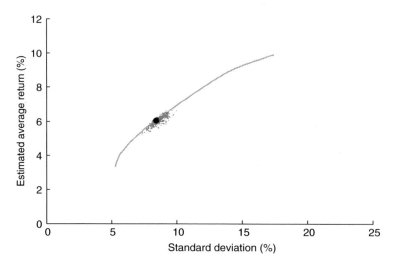

Exhibit 7.1 Resampled Efficiency and Associated Efficient Portfolios

weight distributions.[11] The trading rule is interpretable as the likelihood that a portfolio will perform similarly to the desired optimal in the investment (out-of-sample) period.

PORTFOLIO MONITORING AND ANALYSIS

The RE optimization rebalancing process also provides a rigorous statistical framework for portfolio monitoring and asset importance analysis. Suppose an asset such as the S&P 500 index is a member of the optimization universe. Then every meta-resampled RE optimal portfolio associated with a given REF portfolio has an allocation to the asset. The REF portfolio is an average of all the simulated associated efficient portfolios. Consequently, for any asset, there is a set of simulated optimal allocations associated with the average REF allocation. This means that various statistics, such as the standard deviation of the average allocation, and percentile values, can be calculated on an asset-by-asset basis.

Exhibit 7.2 provides a meta-resampled asset-by-asset statistical distribution analysis of a given (middle) REF portfolio. The hatch marks refer to the REF optimal asset allocations at this particular point on the frontier. The bars represent the 25th/75th percentile ranges of the allocations.[12] The results are presented in tabular form in Table 7.1. The second column is the REF asset allocation; the fourth and fifth columns indicate

11. The Britten-Jones (1999) range estimates of optimized portfolio weights use the unbounded MV optimization framework. RE results have less variance as well as different coefficients.
12. Standard deviations may also be displayed. Percentile ranges are often more useful in practice.

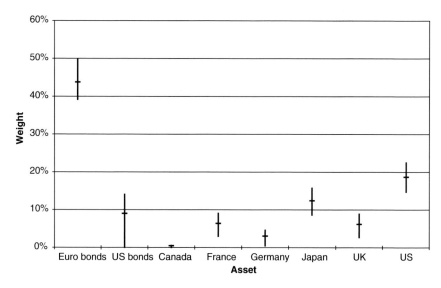

Exhibit 7.2 Portfolio Bounds (25th/75th Percentile Asset Weight Ranges)

the 25th and 75th percentile estimates for the REF asset allocations. The third column is the standard error of the RE optimized weight for the 500 simulations used in the computation. The standard error is useful to understand how much error may exist in the simulation computation for each REF asset allocation.

Exhibit 7.2 and Table 7.1 are very useful portfolio management tools. One application is portfolio monitoring. If the current portfolio has asset weights that range outside the percentile bars in Exhibit 7.2, rebalancing to optimality may be advisable. Note that the ranges vary by assets. The percentile ranges can be compared to the incorrect ad hoc fixed-range rules in current practice. Note also that optimal portfolio weight magnitude may often be independent of statistical significance. For example, in Exhibit 7.2, U.S. bonds have a larger allocation than U.K. equity, but the U.K. equity allocation is statistically significant while the U.S. bonds allocation is not.

Statistical significance of an asset is another important application of the meta-resampled probability rule. It identifies which assets are important and which are not. Note that the meta-resampled asset importance procedure is an enhancement of the ad hoc partial derivative rules in common use in equity portfolio optimization. Statistical significance, and not partial derivatives, is the proper method of determining importance in an optimization. The procedure can also be used to enhance the Sharpe (1992) returns-based style analysis procedure by including statistical estimates of the significance of the style coefficients.

Table 7.1 RE Optimal Middle Portfolio and Statistics

Assets	REF Optimal Portfolio	Standard Error	25th Percentile	75th Percentile
Euro Bonds	44%	0.7%	40%	50%
US Bonds	9%	0.9%	0%	14%
Canada	0%	0.1%	0%	0%
France	6%	0.4%	3%	9%
Germany	3%	0.3%	0%	5%
Japan	12%	0.5%	9%	16%
UK	6%	0.4%	3%	9%
US	19%	0.6%	15%	23%

CONCLUSION

Resampling provides an important route for understanding the statistical characteristics of linear constrained MV optimized portfolios with uncertainty. RE optimization methods lead to the first statistically rigorous and effective portfolio trading rule. Resampling also provides the first rigorous yet easy-to-apply portfolio monitoring framework and asset importance analysis. The RE optimal rebalancing rule often leads to sharp changes in institutional trading policies. RE asset analysis often shows that allocation size and importance are not closely related. Proper application of the RE statistical rules makes available new fundamental and reliable practices for improved asset management.

APPENDIX: CONFIDENCE REGION FOR THE SAMPLE MEAN VECTOR

The computation of a confidence region for a sample mean vector often assumes a random sample of vectors from a multivariate normal distribution (Johnson & Wichern, 1992, chapter 5). In this case, the sample mean vector has an F distribution with p and $n - p$ degrees of freedom, where p denotes the rank of the covariance matrix and n the number of random samples. If the sample size is large enough, the distribution is approximately multivariate normal and the F distribution is applicable. The test statistic for the vector of the sample mean is as follows:

$$(\bar{x} - \mu_0)'^* \Sigma^{-1*}(\bar{x} - \mu_0) \leq \text{constant}. \tag{7A.1}$$

Here, $\bar{x}$ is the sample mean vector of the random vectors and Σ is the sample covariance matrix of random vectors. The distribution of the statistic in formula (7A.1) is an F distribution dependent on the number of observations and degrees of freedom or rank of the positive definite covariance matrix. Formula (7A.1) is interpretable as a normalized distance function of the sample mean vector. The simultaneous confidence interval is the collection of vectors that satisfy (7A.1).

Suppose a two-asset optimization with only a budget constraint. The confidence region centered at the resampled efficient portfolio is, in general, the area contained in a tilted ellipse, where the tilt depends on the correlation of return between the two assets. For portfolios with three or more assets, the values of the portfolio weights that lie in a resampled efficient frontier confidence region have an N-dimensional ellipsoid geometry that is often hard to visualize.

For the resampled efficient frontier, the portfolio weights from the resampled MV efficient portfolios define the sample mean vector and covariance matrix. The budget constraint reduces the rank of the covariance matrix by 1. For sign-constrained efficient portfolios, additional issues arise. For example, the sign constraint leads to a minimum variance resampled portfolio in Table 6.1 that depends largely on the return of one asset. In this case, sign constraints may significantly reduce the rank of the portfolio covariance matrix. Consequently, the assumptions of the test statistic (7A.1), as applied to resampled MV efficient frontier portfolios, are invalid.

8

Input Estimation and Stein Estimators

The investment value of optimized portfolios depends on proper input estimation as well as effective portfolio optimization. For many analysts and investors, input estimation methods may seem a largely settled and uncontroversial issue. Managers usually base asset allocation risk-return estimates on sample means, standard deviations, and correlations computed from historic returns, with adjustments for current information. Institutional equity portfolio optimization generally employs commercial risk measurement services for estimating the components of portfolio risk and advanced statistical methods for computing return.

Contemporary professional statisticians use a variety of modern statistical techniques that are designed to improve the forecast value of estimates of risk and return from historic data.[1] Many of these new procedures are based on results that indicate current investment practice may be suboptimal. These results are particularly important because investment intuition is unreliable. Portfolio optimization requires multivariate statistical estimation; that is, the simultaneous estimation of means, standard deviations, and correlations for many securities. Since financial assets are generally related to each other, there is likely to be information in the group of returns that can improve parameter estimates for each asset.

---

1. Examples include Jobson, Korkie, and Ratti (1979, 1980) and Jobson and Korkie (1981), who use James-Stein (1961) estimation to improve MV optimization, and others mentioned in this chapter.

This chapter is devoted to the discussion of Stein estimators for improving portfolio optimization inputs.[2] These procedures are designed to use group information to improve the forecast value of estimates. Properly used, Stein methods may enhance optimization estimates and lead to more intuitive optimized portfolios. Stein estimation also provides a framework for additional tests of the out-of-sample performance of RE versus MV optimization.

ADMISSIBLE ESTIMATORS

The concept of admissibility is an important one in modern statistical estimation. A statistic is said to be admissible if no other statistic is always better.[3] Intuitively, admissibility is a minimal condition for using a statistic to estimate a parameter. The reader may wonder why anyone uses a statistic that is not admissible; however, the investment community often does.

Charles Stein (1955) astonished the scientific community by proving that sample means are not an admissible statistic for a multivariate population mean under very general conditions. Stein's result implies that there are uniformly better methods for estimating optimization means than the sample mean in many cases. Though these results appeared more than 45 years ago, financial economists and investment practitioners have often ignored methods that have the potential of improving optimization parameter estimation.[4] Interestingly, financial economists and investment practitioners are not alone.[5]

BAYESIAN PROCEDURES AND PRIORS

Many of the most powerful methods in modern statistics are Bayesian. Bayesian statistics generally differ from standard frequentist statistics in that they apply outside beliefs and structure to statistical estimates. Stein estimators are examples of Bayesian statistical estimation procedures. Bayesian procedures assume a prior. A prior is either a reasonable guess at the answer or an assumption that imposes exogenous structure on potential solutions. Stein estimators differ from more general Bayesian estimators in that the prior is designed to be generally applicable for a wide range of estimation contexts. Stein methods transform the optimization by imposing structure on the forecasts to lower the estimation error in sample statistics and reduce dependence on pure statistically estimated data. Bayesian procedures are fundamentally the basis of most of the proposed techniques for improving MV optimization.

---

2. The methods are named after Charles Stein, a pioneer of modern multivariate statistical estimation.
3. More precisely, an estimator is admissible if no other estimator is uniformly better for a given loss function.
4. For example, James and Stein (1961).
5. See Efron and Morris (1975) and Copas (1983) for discussions of some of the Stein estimator controversy.

It should be noted that the development of admissible Stein estimators for optimization input estimation is an area of ongoing research.
With some exceptions, Stein estimators were not developed with financial
applications in mind. An appropriate prior is an important issue in any
application. Chapters 9 and 10 discuss additional applications of Bayesian
procedures in investment contexts of interest.

FOUR STEIN ESTIMATORS

Stein estimators are generally "shrinkage" operators. The amount of
"shrinkage" depends on the consistency of the prior with sample data.
Stein estimators generally work by producing a posterior estimate, which
is a combination of observed history and the Bayesian prior. For example,
a Stein estimator of asset means will tend to shrink sample means more
toward the prior when they are dissimilar than when they are not. The
prior provides an anchor to the estimation process that tends to reduce
estimation ambiguity while increasing forecast value.

A number of Stein estimators are available for MV optimization estimation.[6] These include the James-Stein (1961), Frost-Savarino (1986), Ledoit
(1994, 1997), and Stein (1982) estimators. The James-Stein procedure is an
estimator for asset means. The Frost-Savarino procedure is a joint estimator of the means and covariances. The Ledoit and Stein procedures are
estimators for the covariance matrix.

JAMES-STEIN ESTIMATOR

The James-Stein estimator for the means is the most widely known Stein
estimator.[7] Since the formula is designed for wide applicability, it is of
interest to discuss it in some detail. The Stein estimator formula of the
mean of asset i, $\hat{\mu}_i$, is:

$$\hat{\mu}_i = \bar{x} + c_i \, (\bar{x}_i - \bar{x}) \tag{8.1}$$

Where $\bar{x}$ = global sample mean, $\bar{x}_i$ = sample mean of asset i, $c_i \geq 0$ and ≤ 1.[8]

This estimator shrinks the sample mean $\bar{x}_i$ to the global mean, $\bar{x}$,
depending on asset variance, σ_i^2. Shrinkage increases as a function
of distance from the global mean and asset variability and decreases
with the number of historical observations.[9] When an observed historical
mean is determined to be sufficiently unreliable (due to a high standard
error), it is shrunk to the global mean. Alternatively, if a historic mean

6. Some early applications to MV optimization include Jorion (1986) and Brown (1976).
7. There are some closely related versions. The one that may be most useful for MV optimization is the
positive rule empirical James-Stein estimator that allows for unequal variances and assumes a global
equal mean prior (Efron & Morris, 1977, p. 123).

8. $c_i = \max\{0, 1 - (k - 3) \, \sigma_i^2 / \Sigma \, (\bar{x}_i - \bar{x})^2)\}$, k = number of assets, $k \geq 3$, σ_i^2 = asset i variance
9. See also Efron and Morris (1973).

Table 8.1 Monthly Dollar (Net) James-Stein Returns (Percentages)

	Euro Bonds	US Bonds	Canada	France	Germany	Japan	UK	US
Mean	0.30	0.31	0.59	0.59	0.59	0.59	0.59	0.60
Standard Deviation	1.56	2.00	5.50	7.03	6.22	7.04	6.01	4.30

has a very small error estimate, the posterior will be very close to historic value.

The James-Stein estimator for the mean may have a significant effect on optimization inputs and results. Consider the return premium data of the base case (Table 2.3). The monthly global mean is 0.59% (7.0% annualized). Many of the equity assets deviate significantly from the global mean and have large standard deviations. Consequently, they are candidates for significant shrinkage. On the other hand, although bond assets have an average return that also deviates substantially from the global mean, the level of variability is less and shrinkage to the global mean is less.

Table 8.1 displays the James-Stein estimates of monthly average return premiums corresponding to Table 2.3. For convenience, Table 8.1 duplicates the monthly standard deviations. Note that the James-Stein procedure shrinks five of the six equity average returns to the global mean.[10]

The James-Stein procedure highlights the substantial volatility and ambiguity implicit in the data in Table 2.3. The estimator in Table 8.1 radically alters perception of information in the historic data and conveys interesting investment implications. One interpretation is that, given the level of variability, the relatively large average returns of many equity asset classes are likely to be unreliable forecasts of future performance.

JAMES-STEIN MV EFFICIENCY

James-Stein estimation often leads to very different MV and RE frontiers. Exhibit 8.1 displays the MV and RE efficient frontiers that result from replacing the historical sample means with the James-Stein estimates in Table 8.1. Exhibit 8.1 provides the MV and RE composition maps for the James-Stein RE optimal portfolios.

The efficient frontiers in Exhibit 8.1 can be directly compared to Exhibit 6.2. Exhibit 8.2 indicates that the composition of the MV and RE efficient portfolios is very much affected by James-Stein estimation. In the MV efficiency case, the U.S. dominates at high risk.

---

10. One alternative is to shrink the equity assets separately from the bond assets since the level of variability is so different. However, in this case, the James-Stein estimator leads to shrinkage to the global mean for all equity assets. The Table 8.1 results seem preferable from a number of perspectives.

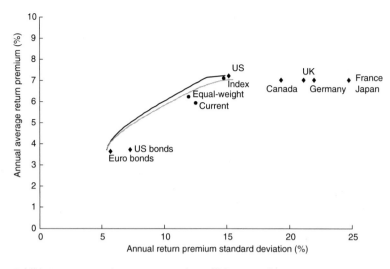

Exhibit 8.1 James-Stein Means MV and RE Efficient Frontiers

OUT-OF-SAMPLE JAMES-STEIN ESTIMATION

The James-Stein estimates of optimization input parameters are designed to be closer to true population values out-of-sample than traditional sample means. This observation suggests a test of the out-of-sample investment value of RE compared to MV efficient frontiers using James-Stein estimation. As the discussion in Chapter 5 noted, the amount of estimation error in the base case data set is much less than in the Jobson and Korkie (1981) data. To use more realistic levels of estimation error, the James-Stein estimates of return assume 10 rather than 18 years of simulated monthly returns in the simulation proof framework of Chapter 6. The

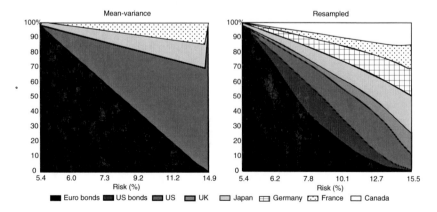

Exhibit 8.2 James-Stein MV and RE Composition Maps

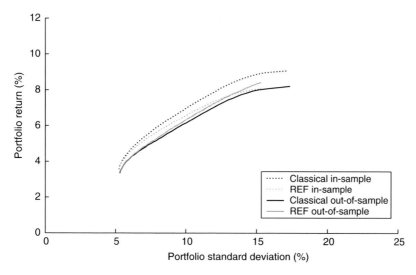

Exhibit 8.3 MV and RE Frontiers with James-Stein Mean Adjustment

in-sample and out-of-sample results are displayed in Exhibit 8.3. As in prior studies, the dotted curves represent in-sample and the solid curves represent out-of-sample average frontier portfolios.

The results in Exhibit 8.3 can be compared to those in Exhibit 6.3. Exhibit 8.3 shows that the in-sample and out-of-sample MV and RE frontiers for the James-Stein estimated data are far closer to each other than in Exhibit 6.3. In other words, James-Stein estimation results in closer agreement of what-you-see in-sample relative to what-you-get on average out-of-sample for MV and RE optimization.[11] However, the tests also show that what-you-see with RE optimization and James-Stein estimation can be very similar to what-you-get on average out-of-sample, particularly at higher levels of risk. Risk level differences are easily explained: James-Stein estimation has little effect at low risk because efficient assets have little variability but more effect at higher risk levels with more variable efficient assets. The potential similarity of in-sample versus out-of-sample RE optimized James-Stein estimated optimized portfolios may be very useful for long-term financial planning applications and equity portfolio optimization where estimated return is measured relative to cost of trading.

FROST-SAVARINO ESTIMATOR

The Frost and Savarino (1986) estimator is one of the most interesting proposed for MV optimization. Notably, it is a joint estimator of the

---

11. Similar results are reported in Jobson and Korkie (1981).

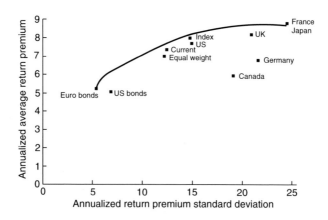

Exhibit 8.4 Frost-Savarino MV Efficient Frontier

means and covariances. The prior is the efficiency of an equal-weighted portfolio.

Exhibit 8.4 illustrates the Frost-Savarino MV efficient frontier for the data in Exhibit 2.5. Note that the Frost-Savarino frontier shifts downward and slightly inward at the high-return end and upward and slightly inward at the low-return end. Essentially, the Frost-Savarino frontier shrinks toward the equal-weighted portfolio. The procedure generally has less impact on MV optimization inputs than the James-Stein estimator.

Frost-Savarino Stein estimation has many attractive properties conceptually. It is the only procedure that estimates all the MV optimization parameters in a unified framework, an approach that seems most appropriate for portfolio optimization. It is a less severe adjustment of optimization inputs than James-Stein. On the other hand, the procedure has significant limitations. The equal-weighted portfolio prior is often not investment relevant in practical applications. In addition, the algorithm is not very numerically stable. Optimizations consisting of 50 or more assets may be difficult to compute. Frost-Savarino estimation is even more computationally intensive when used in conjunction with Monte Carlo simulation procedures and REF estimation.

COVARIANCE ESTIMATION

The covariance matrix is a summary of the risk estimates associated with assets in an MV optimization.[12]

Asset allocation studies often estimate the sample covariance matrix with historic return data, as in tables 2.3 and 2.4. Commercial equity

12. The covariance matrix is square with n rows and columns equal to the number of assets. The (i,j) element is the covariance of the ith and j^{th} assets. It follows that the ith diagonal element is equal to the variance of the ith asset.

portfolio risk services typically use factor models and advanced statistical techniques to estimate the components of portfolio risk. Multivariate equity risk estimation addresses the particular needs of optimizing large institutional portfolios and communicating with clients. The analysis of equity risk estimation is a substantial endeavor beyond the scope of this text and constitutes a significant digression from the study of MV optimization.[13]

Asset managers have typically ignored Stein methods for covariance estimation. Conventional wisdom has it that risk estimation is a second-order consideration for portfolio optimization relative to forecasting return. Unfortunately, conventional wisdom may be in serious error in important instances. There are two issues associated with covariance estimation that directly affect the value of optimized portfolios: (1) existence of sufficient data for well-conditioned covariance estimation and (2) impact of estimation error on covariance estimation.

Conceptually, covariance estimation requires substantially more data than are usually available for portfolio optimization. Optimizing N assets requires N time periods of observed returns.[14] If insufficient data are available, the covariance matrix is singular and proper portfolio optimization infeasible.[15] However, much more data are typically required to avoid ill conditioning. An ill-conditioned covariance matrix is often a serious cause of MV optimization instability (Michaud, 1989a).[16]

Increasing the number of assets has another estimation error effect on portfolio optimization. While increasing the number of assets increases estimation error in return estimation linearly, it increases estimation error in the covariance matrix quadratically. For a sufficiently large number of assets, the accumulation of covariance estimation error may be the dominant factor in the optimization process.[17] Such effects implicitly affect large universe equity portfolio optimizations. In many cases the

---

13. See Rosenberg and McKibben (1973), Rosenberg and Guy (1973), and Rosenberg (1974).

14. Essentially, portfolio optimization requires inverting the covariance matrix. A covariance matrix may be non-singular, and therefore invertible, but not well conditioned. In this case the optimization is very unstable. As a rule of thumb, the number of time periods observed should be an order of magnitude more than the number of securities in the optimization universe.

15. Unfortunately, many commercially available optimizers have unsophisticated algorithms and are insensitive to whether or not the covariance matrix is properly defined. Such an optimizer should be avoided since it will attempt to invest in investment nonsense such as positions with zero or even negative estimated risk.

16. Technically, ill conditioning amounts to having a large ratio of the largest to smallest eigenvalue associated with the sample covariance matrix. The consequence of this large ratio is to effectively amplify the (potentially small) errors in the estimated return series by a very large factor; that factor being the so-called condition number of the sample covariance matrix. The base case data covariance matrix condition number is 530, indicating significant instability and ill conditioning. Additionally, a so-called discretization error is also to blame for such increased instability in the MV optimization. Specifically, keeping all other things the same, increasing the number of assets in the MV optimization problem increases the resulting condition number of the covariance matrix, rendering the MV optimization problem more difficult and less stable.

17. Personal communication from Philippe Jorion, May 1996.

problems of insufficient data and the accumulation of estimation errors are unrecognized, leading to unstable optimizations and irrelevant portfolios. Only recently have Stein covariance estimation methods become available that address some of these important issues.

STEIN COVARIANCE ESTIMATION

Ledoit (1994, 1997) developed Stein estimation methods for the sample covariance matrix. The Ledoit estimator is a general procedure for optimally shrinking the covariance matrix toward a prior.[18] Notably, the Ledoit estimator uses the Sharpe (1964)-Lintner (1965) capital asset pricing model (CAPM) as a prior for estimating risk. The CAPM prior, arguably the most appropriate for understanding risk for financial data, assumes assets are correlated to each other only through their sensitivity to the market by a linear relationship between systematic risk and return.

The Ledoit estimator has many attractive properties for finance. As Ledoit shows, the estimator significantly improves sample covariance estimation and reduces instability in MV optimization in the context of classic financial data. It is also the first covariance estimation procedure to allow robust estimation of the full covariance matrix even if the number of assets exceeds the number of observations. In addition, the procedure is very flexible and has the potential to be used with other alternative priors.

Another Stein estimator of the covariance matrix was developed by Stein (1982) and Dey and Srinivasan (1985). Their procedure is a minimax estimator similar in important ways to Ledoit.[19] Using Monte Carlo simulation, Ledoit (1994) finds that both Stein estimators may significantly improve sample covariance estimation and the stability of MV optimization.

Stein estimators help when standard errors are large. If there are many observations, or the number of assets is small, the benefits of the Ledoit and minimax estimators may be relatively minimal. For the historic data of tables 2.3 and 2.4, neither estimator significantly alters the sample covariance matrix or the optimization results. Ledoit estimates that the benefits of his covariance estimator kick in when the number of assets and periods reach 30.[20] One area of significant application may be to global equity portfolio optimization, where the number of assets can be very large and the number of historic periods of useful data is often small. Because the Ledoit estimator may be useful in situations with

---

18. See the appendix to this chapter for further, more technical discussion.
19. In both cases, the sample covariance shrinks toward a prior. In the Stein-Dey-Srinivasan case, the estimator is minimax; that is, no other estimator has lower worst-case error. This is in contrast to the Ledoit estimator, which uses square error loss (Hilbert-Schmidt or Frobenius norm).
20. The benefits depend on the ratio of the assets to periods as well as to the prior.

minimal historic data, applications to short-term asset allocation may evolve over time.

Stein covariance estimation may also be useful for asset management by improving regression estimates of equity risk and return forecasts. Generalized least squares (GLS) regression is more powerful and robust in many applications relevant to investment management (Kandel & Stambaugh, 1995). Ledoit shows that his covariance estimator used in the context of GLS regression may significantly change the factor-return relationships observed in some well-known empirical studies.[21] Other Stein estimators designed to improve the forecast power of linear regression estimation are also available. In particular, the James-Stein linear regression estimator is widely used by many working econometricians.[22]

UTILITY FUNCTIONS AND INPUT ESTIMATION

The reader may have noted that Bayesian priors as applied to utility function-based optimization have been ignored in our discussion of input estimation. This may seem surprising because many of the early studies on estimation error and its impact on MV optimization applied Bayesian priors to utility functions.[23] One reason they are not addressed here is the practical problem of utility function specificity discussed in Chapter 3. In addition, as Barry (1974) notes, although the optimal portfolio chosen by Bayesian estimation methods applied to utility functions may vary, the efficient frontier composition may not change. Procedures that leave the efficient frontier portfolios unaltered are likely to have limited practical investment value.

AD HOC ESTIMATORS

There are a number of ad hoc estimators of the covariance matrix. Perhaps the best known is Sharpe's (1963) single-index model. There are also multi-index and equal-correlation models. Such methods provide simple approaches to estimating risk and the covariance matrix. They may have practical value when the number of observations is small relative to the number of assets and the alternative is a singular covariance matrix. Historically, ad hoc procedures have often been the only ones available for dealing with many limitations of investment data. However, as Ledoit (1994) notes, such procedures may impose arbitrary structure and ignore information available in historic data. The Stein covariance estimation methods are conceptually superior. Properly formulated Stein methods ignore neither reasonable structure nor information in historic data. Such

---

21. Ledoit (1994) repeats Fama-French (1992) and finds that beta is now nearly significant.
22. Judge et al. (1988, pp. 836–838) discuss Stein rules for multivariate linear regression.
23. For example Bawa et al. (1979).

estimators weight the prior and data optimally to produce superior risk estimation. Although ad hoc methods have the virtue of simplicity and familiarity, they may be inferior to well-defined Stein estimators, when available.

STEIN ESTIMATION CAVEATS

In Chapter 6 asset allocation studies, sign constraints reflect an all-assets-investable prior. Sign constraints provide investment-relevant direction for computing MV and RE optimized portfolios. In the simulation studies in the text, the base case data set is assumed as the truth. In general, base case data reflect increased return with increased risk and are not strictly consistent with the James-Stein "all assets equal" prior.[24] The example illustrates the fact that Stein estimation priors may be inconsistent with optimization constraint priors and the combination may not be additive.[25] While in practice truth and level of estimation error are unknown, an analyst should be vigilant that Stein estimation priors are consistent with optimization constraint priors in order to benefit from RE optimization.

CONCLUSIONS

Stein estimators represent an important set of procedures for improving the practical value of MV optimization. Rationalizing the use of inadmissible estimators for the mean or covariance in practice is often difficult when financially relevant alternatives are available. It is also increasingly hard to rationalize ad hoc estimators used by many investment practitioners. On the other hand, the development of Stein estimators for portfolio optimization is at an early stage. In particular, the identification of the optimal Stein estimator in many practical investment contexts remains open. In addition, Stein estimation priors may be inconsistent with constraint priors implicit in RE portfolio optimization and may not be additive. The investment community has a strong vested interest in encouraging further research in the area of Stein estimators with financially relevant investment priors.

APPENDIX: LEDOIT COVARIANCE ESTIMATION

If the sample covariance matrix has rank N, where N is the number of assets, then the matrix will have N positive eigenvalues. For the historic data in tables 2.3 and 2.4, the eight eigenvalues corresponding to the

24. Robert Michaud has developed a CAPM-prior James-Stein estimate of return.
25. Another possible example is the Ledoit CAPM prior estimator in an index-relative optimization.

eight asset classes range from 0.23 to 121.6. The eigenvalues of a matrix are often useful in understanding its statistical characteristics.[26]

Ledoit (1994) demonstrates that stability of the optimization depends on statistical properties of the eigenvalues of the covariance matrix. In particular, the ill conditioning of the sample covariance matrix is attributable to a small eigenvalues bias toward zero. The bias increases as the number of assets increases relative to the number of periods. Improved covariance estimation requires pushing the small eigenvalues away from zero while shrinking the large ones toward an appropriate prior. The Ledoit procedure is not a specific estimator but may allow many alternative financial priors.

---

26. For a useful brief introduction into properties of matrices, including eigenvalues and eigenvectors, see Johnson and Wichern (1992, Chapter 2).

9

Benchmark Mean-Variance Optimization

Benchmarks arise naturally in many asset management contexts. For example, an equity manager's performance is typically evaluated relative to the return and tracking risk of an index such as the S&P 500. Tactical asset allocation performance is generally measured relative to a return index. Investment policy asset allocation may be associated with funding an appropriate return liability.[1]

This chapter addresses MV optimization relative to a return index or benchmark. The benchmark redefines risk in terms of the return of an investment-relevant objective. Mathematically, benchmark-relative optimization is MV optimization with a linear equality constraint representing the benchmark.[2] Benchmark-relative optimization without linear inequality constraints, such as sign constraints, is subject to the same estimation error investment limitations as described in Jobson and Korkie (1980, 1981) and discussed in Chapter 4. While MV optimization relative to a benchmark may reduce instability at low risk, the statistical significance of investment information may be diminished.

BENCHMARK-RELATIVE OPTIMIZATION CHARACTERISTICS

Traditional sign-constrained benchmark-relative MV optimization displayed in Exhibit 2.2 is based on residual risk-return estimates relative to

---

1. We address benchmark optimization in the context of a return liability for financial intermediaries more specifically in Chapter 10.
2. Sum of active weights equals zero.

Table 9.1 Monthly Dollar (Net) Index-Relative Returns (Percentages), 01/78–12/95

	Euro Bonds	US Bonds	Canada	France	Germany	Japan	UK	US
Mean	−0.48	−0.51	−0.36	0.13	−0.22	0.13	0.04	−0.04
Standard Deviation	3.92	4.05	4.31	4.90	4.81	4.63	4.06	3.21

the difference between asset and benchmark return.[3] By definition, the benchmark portfolio is MV residual return efficient.[4]

Assume the data of tables 2.3 and 2.4 and the index portfolio defined in Table 2.2. Table 9.1 displays the monthly means and standard deviations of index-relative return for the eight asset classes. While average returns simply reflect a constant shift in value, risk has changed.[5] For example, while Japan and France are, as before, nearly equal in return, index-relative risk for Japan is significantly less than France because it is a larger component of the index in Table 2.2. The residual risk-return estimates and sign constraints result in the efficient frontier in Exhibit 2.2.

TRACKING ERROR OPTIMIZATION AND CONSTRAINTS

Institutional equity portfolio investment mandates are typically defined as maximizing residual or index-relative return for a given level of residual or tracking error risk. The composition of the index is assumed known with certainty. MV index-relative portfolio optimizations are typically long only; that is, sign constraints on asset weights are assumed. This is because investors often want to avoid unlimited liability investments. The sign-constrained efficient frontier in Exhibit 2.2 represents the index-relative optimization framework of choice for many asset allocation studies and equity portfolio strategies.

Investment managers often add additional constraints to a MV optimization in an attempt to improve out-of-sample investment performance.[6] As noted in Chapter 6, sign constraints may reflect a valuable Bayesian prior for defining optimality in a non-index-relative RE optimization in the

---

3. For an index return benchmark, there are three equivalent ways of defining index-relative MV optimization. When the optimization inputs are defined as index-relative or residual returns, either active portfolio weights (sum to zero) or portfolio weights (sum to 1) MV optimization is equivalent because the index has no risk and no return. Alternatively, MV optimization based on the original optimization inputs with active weight constraints is also equivalent. This is the approach taken in Roll (1992).
4. The issue of whether the benchmark is or is not MV efficient on an absolute return basis and its implications is discussed further in the section on Roll's (1992) analysis.
5. The correlations are also changed.
6. Other reasons for constraints include legal restrictions, investment mandates, and ad hoc marketability.

context of estimation error.[7] Investment-relevant optimization constraints
provide useful direction to the uncertainty represented in the resampled
MV optimization averaging process for defining enhanced optimality.[8]
However, in an index-relative context, sign constraints may reflect perverse constraint priors for RE optimization. For example, from Table 9.1,
sign constraints imply that bonds are desirable index-relative investments, contradicting their large negative residual returns.

Asset investability depends on willingness to under- or over-weight
assets relative to index weights. Index-relative returns can be used to
formulate active weight sign constraints.[9] In Table 9.1, Euro bonds, U.S.
bonds, Canada, and Germany have relatively large negative residual
returns. An optimal portfolio is unlikely to have positive active weights
for these assets, all other things the same. Similarly, an optimal portfolio
is unlikely to have negative asset weights for France and Japan. On the
other hand, the U.S. and U.K. residual returns are relatively small and
risk is moderate. An active weight sign prior for U.K. and U.S. equities
may be undesirable. It is difficult to anticipate optimized active weight
sign for these two assets because the value of risk reduction versus return
enhancement may vary over the efficient frontier. Table 9.2 summarizes
a set of constraints reflecting reasonable active weight sign priors for the
index-relative MV optimization data in Table 9.1. Note that all assets are
sign constrained.[10]

The Chapter 6 simulation framework is applied to compare traditional sign-constrained index-relative MV optimization relative to active
weights-constrained index-relative RE optimized portfolios. The simulation truth is the sign-constrained MV efficient frontier based on Table
9.1 data. The dotted curves in Exhibit 9.1 display the average in-sample
simulated efficient frontiers, the solid curves the out-of-sample average
performance. The dotted black curve is the in-sample MV index-relative

Table 9.2 Index-Relative Constraint Priors

	Euro Bonds	US Bonds	Canada	France	Germany	Japan	UK	US
Min	0%	0%	0%	10%	0%	30%	0%	0%
Max	0%	0%	5%	100%	10%	100%	100%	100%

7. The discussion teaches that thoughtful non-ad hoc (economically meaningful) constraints are your
friends and should always be included. Note how the unbounded MV optimization framework ignoring estimation error in Clarke et al. (2002, 2006) leads to very different conclusions.

8. Excluding, of course, constraints that are investment mandated, legally imposed, and ad hoc based.

9. Bayesian prior constraints may also be based on statistical significance rather than the sign of index-
relative return. For example, the information ratio can be used to dichotomize positive, negative, and
insignificant index-relative constrained assets. Other methods that include correlations may also be
desirable.

10. We turn to long-short investing later in the chapter.

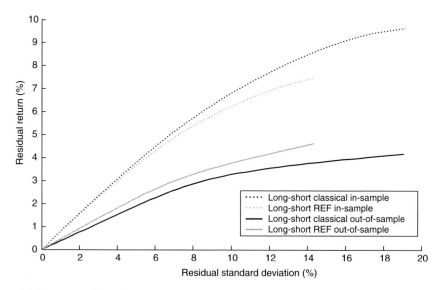

Exhibit 9.1 In- and Out-of-Sample Index-Relative MV and RE Optimized Portfolios

sign-constrained efficient frontier; the dotted gray curve is the in-sample RE index-relative Table 9.2 constrained efficient frontier. The solid black curve represents the out-of-sample performance on average of the MV efficient portfolios; the solid gray curve represents the out-of-sample performance on average of the RE efficient portfolios.

The in-sample MV efficient frontier expects more estimated return and is willing to bear more risk than the in-sample RE constrained portfolios. This is the familiar error-maximization effect associated with MV optimized portfolios. The lower solid curves teach that the efficient portfolios with active weight sign priors and RE optimization dramatically dominate traditional MV index-relative optimized portfolios out-of-sample. RE optimization, properly managed, may substantially enhance investment performance in an index-relative framework.

Exhibit 9.2 displays the composition maps of the sign-constrained index-relative MV and Table 9.2 constrained RE optimized portfolios. The upper panel is the composition map for index-relative MV optimized portfolios; the lower panel is the composition map for RE optimization. Compared to MV, the RE composition map represents smooth transitions from one level of risk to another and more diversified portfolios at higher levels of risk.

CONSTRAINT ALTERNATIVES

It is of interest to compare the performance of alternative active weight constraints relative to those in Table 9.2. The constraints in Table 9.3 replace sign constraints with active index weight constraints for the U.K. and U.S indices.

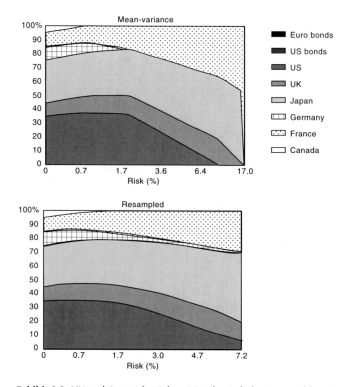

Exhibit 9.2 MV and Constraint Priors RE Index-Relative Composition Maps

Table 9.3 optimizations relative to Exhibit 9.1 are more constrained, resulting in efficient frontiers that have a reduced range of risk but also less error maximization in-sample and similar levels of return at reduced risk out-of-sample. Relative to Table 9.2 constraints, Table 9.3 constrained RE optimizations produce enhanced performance on average within a reduced range of efficient risk.

Another alternative strategy for defining asset weight constraints is to consider assets such as the U.K. and U.S. as representing statistically insignificant index-relative risk-return estimates. A statistically insignificant asset is consistent with assigning an index weight constraint. Assigning index weights to statistically insignificant assets is likely to reduce estimation error and enhance performance while restricting the range of efficient risk.

Table 9.3 Alternative Index Constraint Priors

	Euro Bonds	US Bonds	Canada	France	Germany	Japan	UK	US
Min	0%	0%	0%	10%	0%	30%	10%	0%
Max	0%	0%	5%	100%	10%	100%	100%	35%

The issue of statistically insignificant optimization information is particularly pervasive in index-relative equity portfolio MV optimizations for large stock indices. Equity portfolio managers often have statistically significant information for only a relatively small number of stocks. Statistically insignificant information implies large estimation error and reduced investment value of optimized portfolios, all other things the same.

Michaud and Michaud (2005a) propose the use of a "composite asset" as a general way of dealing with insignificant information in an index-relative equity portfolio RE optimization. A composite asset is defined as an index-weighted asset of all insignificant information assets in the optimization universe. The procedure redefines the optimization universe in terms of statistically significant assets and the composite asset. The benefits include reduced estimation error while maintaining index representativeness and tracking error risk control.

ROLL'S ANALYSIS

There are a wide variety of indices proposed for index-relative tracking error MV optimization mandates. The indices may vary from standard capital market indices such as the S&P 500 to sectors, industries, and hybrid asset classes. From the manager's point of view, the index defines the investment objective and little consideration may be given to the investment relevance of the index. However, investors and trustees have a stake in whether financial characteristics of the index may limit investment value.

Roll (1992) provides an important theoretical analysis of the index-relative efficient frontier framework. He demonstrates that many portfolios not on the index-relative MV efficient frontier may dominate index-relative efficient portfolios if the index is not MV efficient. Roll's concern is that the convenience of an index-relative efficient frontier framework for asset management may come at too high a price in terms of suboptimal investment.

Roll's valuable cautionary analysis teaches us to avoid ad hoc indices in index-relative optimization.[11] The theoretical limitations of the index-relative framework diminish in practice as the MV efficiency and economic representativeness of the benchmark increase. Roll notes in his conclusion (1992, pp. 19–20) that the problem with the suboptimality of the index-relative MV efficiency framework may need to be balanced against the impact of estimation error on MV optimization in the classic framework.

INDEX EFFICIENCY

The technology developed in Chapter 7 provides a basis for measuring the statistical MV efficiency of an index portfolio. Table 9.4 compares the (sign-constrained) index portfolio defined in Table 2.2 to the similar risk

---

11. See also Kandel and Stambaugh (1995) and Roll and Ross (1994).

Table 9.4 Index vs. Risk-Similar RE Optimal Portfolio

	Euro Bonds	US Bonds	Canada	France	Germany	Japan	UK	US
Index	0.0%	0.0%	5.0%	10.0%	10.0%	30.0%	10.0%	35.0%
RE Opt	2.9%	1.8%	1.2%	17.9%	4.6%	25.3%	15.6%	30.7%

level (non-index-relative sign-constrained) RE optimal portfolio from Chapter 6. On inspection the two portfolios seem to have similar portfolio structure. However, the meta-resampled need-to-trade probability measures 20%, an indication of statistically significant differences and suboptimality. Skepticism about the investment value of index-relative MV optimization using the index in Table 2.2 in a practical setting may be warranted.

A SIMPLE BENCHMARK-RELATIVE FRAMEWORK

Imposing general capital market structure on an optimization rather than optimizing to a specific index may be desirable in some cases. For example, in our base case data set, we may wish to include global market structural relationships such as equal U.S. and non-U.S. equity and equal Euro and U.S. bonds. Slack constraints may be imposed to allow the structural relationships to be satisfied within some range of values, such as ±10% of equality. A benchmark-relative framework with slack constraints on investment-relevant structural relationships allows for RE optimization performance enhancement. The slack constraints condition the uncertainty created in the resampling of investment information to define, via the averaging process, improved risk-adjusted MV optimal portfolios on average. The optimized portfolios exhibit the usual desirable REF investment properties of robustness and stability.

An important benefit of the slack constrained RE optimization framework is that it may avoid the Roll critique of possible suboptimal investment solutions. The limitation of the procedure is that it does not satisfy a tracking error risk objective required in many investment mandates. If the index-relative tracking error objective is required, the traditional framework is appropriate. From the investor's point of view, however, concern with the limitations of a suboptimal index on the value of the investment is an important consideration.

LONG-SHORT INVESTING

Traditional sign-constrained index-relative MV optimization is long-short investing without leverage. Increasingly, long-short investing is becoming a standard in institutional equity portfolio management. Prime broker technology and trading systems have reduced costs and made long-short investing economically practical in many cases of investment interest.

Equity portfolio indices such as the S&P 500 index have highly asymmetric index weights. Long-short investment strategies are often proposed to address index asymmetric optimization biases in equity portfolio management.[12] In long-only optimization, index weight asymmetry limits the ability of the manager to use negative information for small index weight stocks; small stocks can only be assigned small negative active weights, while large stocks can be assigned large negative as well as positive active weights in an optimized portfolio. A long-short 120/20 or 130/30 strategy may allow relatively symmetric constraints on stocks in an optimization universe.[13] Two-fund long-short strategies may also limit the impact of index asymmetric constraints on portfolio optimization.[14] A simple alternative that avoids short investing is two-stage optimization; the first stage determines the theoretically optimal portfolio with index-symmetric constraints; the second stage attempts to closely replicate this portfolio while satisfying investability constraints.

Long-short investing may also be of interest in asset allocation studies. For example, in the case of Table 9.2 index-relative constraint priors, since shorts were not allowed, the bond indices are constrained to a zero weight. From an investment perspective the bond indices represent large negative index-relative returns that would likely enhance investment value if shorting were allowed.

Exhibit 9.3 compares the Chapter 6 simulation test of in-sample and out-of-sample index-relative RE and MV long-short optimization. Shorting is allowed for the four large index-relative residual return assets; specifically, the minimum weights are –20% for the bond indices, –15% for Canada, and –10% for Germany. The short minimums are uniformly –20% (left-hand symmetric) from index weights. In the RE optimized portfolios the remaining constraint priors in Table 9.2 are employed. In the MV optimized portfolios, sign constraints are assumed for all other assets up to a maximum of 100%.[15]

Exhibit 9.3 displays the in-sample and out-of-sample RE optimized efficient frontiers for the index-relative long-short constraint priors as described in the prior paragraph relative to the RE optimized frontiers for the Table 9.2 index-relevant sign-constrained priors. The RE optimized

12. Long-short optimized portfolios generally need to satisfy certain conditions (Jacobs et al., 2006a) in order to have practical investment value.
13. See Jacobs and Levy (2006b).
14. In the classical long-short case analyzed in Michaud (1993), before shorting, both the long and short portfolios are sign-constrained, creating relatively symmetric constraints on the total portfolio.
15. This framework is fairly standard for MV long-short index-relative optimization where assets are sign-constrained except for those where shorting is allowed to enhance investment value.

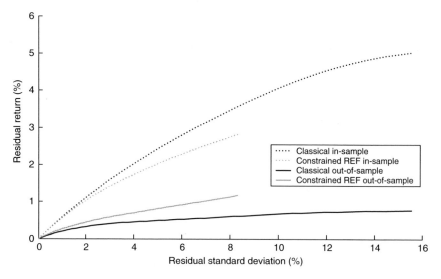

Exhibit 9.3 Average In- and Out-of-Sample Long-Short Index-Relative MV and RE Frontiers

long-short portfolios dominate performance on average relative to the traditional MV long-short portfolios.[16]

CONCLUSION

Index-relative MV optimization has important applications in investment practice. The index portfolio may define the investment mandate or use of invested assets. In many cases the investment mandate is defined to maximize index-relative return relative to a given level of index tracking error risk. Asset investability depends on your willingness to under- or over-weight assets relative to index weights. Sign constraints on asset weights may often reflect a perverse Bayesian prior in an index-relative RE optimization. The resampling process uses index-relevant active weight sign constraints to enhance likely investment performance. RE optimization, properly managed, has the potential for significantly improving index-relative, long-short as well as sign-constrained portfolio optimization. However, as Roll (1992) has shown, the MV efficiency of the index is related to the value of the investment framework. A non-active-weight index-relative framework may provide a useful alternative benchmark relative framework that may avoid the Roll (1992) critique.

---

16. The RE optimized portfolios also dominate out-of-sample MV optimized long-short portfolios with the same RE constraints.

10

Investment Policy and Economic Liabilities

Investment policy is the proposed long-term average risk level or asset allocation stock/bond ratio for the fund. For many trustees, appropriately defining investment policy relative to fund liabilities or use of invested assets is a major priority and significant fiduciary responsibility. An investment policy study often consists of substantial expenditures of time and capital. Many consider investment policy as the single most important investment decision for long-term investors.[1]

Investment policy is generally implemented in a core-satellite framework comprising strategic and tactical asset management mandates. A strategic asset allocation consists of an optimal risk-adjusted portfolio for a particular stock-bond mix policy and rebalancing to maintain that policy. Strategic asset allocations represent a core investment strategy that are generally based on relatively long-term risk-return relationships relative to liquid, diversified, and economically representative fixed and non-fixed income global capital market indices, often implemented with index funds.[2] Long-term investors consider strategic asset allocation funds the investments of choice because they are designed to optimally enhance long-term compound return on a risk-adjusted basis. Tactical funds

---

1. Brinson et al. (1986, 1991) find that the long-term average stock/bond ratio is the single most important factor explaining long-term performance of institutional pension funds. Hensel et al. (1991), using similar data though somewhat different methods, find that investment policy is as important as any investment decision.
2. Index-fund-based Exchange Traded Funds (ETFs) are an increasingly popular alternative particularly for financial advisors and sophisticated individual investors.

of various kinds may be included to enhance return relative to capital market benchmarks. The long-term consequences of risk policy decisions may be computed with specially designed calculators and Monte Carlo simulation studies.[3]

Conceptually, MV optimization is a natural framework for defining investment policy. MV optimizations in a benchmark- or liability-relative framework seem an obvious choice for defining an optimal long-term asset allocation. The index-relative methods of Chapter 9 can be used to develop appropriate optimal portfolios. Beyond the limitations of traditional MV optimization, investment policy studies have the additional burden of defining a financially relevant liability benchmark.

MISUSING OPTIMIZATION

In practice, an MV optimization framework used in defining investment policy is very vulnerable to being misused and overmanaged. Because of instability, MV optimizations are often inconsistent with investment intuition and consensus institutional perceptions unless highly managed. A great deal of pressure exists to find acceptable optimized investment policy allocations. Many constraints and assumptions, rationalized as reflecting institutional objectives, are often part of the optimization process. All too often an investment policy MV optimization study provides little more than a veneer of scientific respectability for rationalizing the recommendations of an ad hoc process.

Because of the importance of the problem, and the limitations of traditional MV optimization, alternative approaches for defining an investment policy have been proposed. The most popular alternative is Monte Carlo financial planning with liability modeling.[4] As discussed in Chapter 3, Monte Carlo asset-liability financial planning in practice is essentially a search algorithm of candidate asset allocations that typically have not been optimized relative to any liability benchmark.

RE optimization with a relevant liability objective has much potential for alleviating many of the important limitations of the MV optimization process for defining investment policy. This chapter focuses on defining the liability in a benchmark-relative optimization framework.

ECONOMIC LIABILITY MODELS

An MV efficiency liability-relative optimization is conceptually a useful framework for defining investment policy in many cases of practical interest (Michaud, 1989c). The optimization procedure requires an investment

---

3. An institutional quality calculator for computing the long-term implications of investment decisions is available from New Frontier Advisors LLC. See Michaud (1981, 2003) for a description of theory and estimation procedures and Michaud et al. (2006a, 2006b) for long-term strategic risk-return estimation.
4. For example, Michaud (1976).

policy-relevant prior in the form of an economic model of fund liabilities or obligations (Michaud, 1989b).

The objective of economic liability modeling is to describe how fund values and obligations interact and change dynamically in time. The economic liability model reflects changes in the fund's obligations as a function of changes in economic factors and asset returns. The economic model may also be a function of the level of assets and liabilities when not equal in value. The success of the procedure depends critically on a valid model of liability risk. An economic liability-relative optimization may radically alter the investment character and value of investment policy recommendations.

Financial intermediary liabilities often have a substantial beta relative to equity capital market indices. This is because intermediary liability risk is often related to maintaining competitiveness relative to similar institutions. For example, an important objective of many college endowment funds is to promote and maintain competitiveness with similar educational institutions relative to the ability to recruit and retain desirable students and faculty. Similarly, an important purpose of a corporate pension plan is to maintain competitiveness for recruiting and retaining desirable employees relative to similar firms. If equity investment volatility affects all competing institutions similarly, there may be little change in the ability of the intermediary to remain competitive and little liability-relative risk for investing in equities.

The notion of an "economic" liability is increasingly accepted as the appropriate definition for defining liability-relative risk. The term *economic* is used to highlight the substantive differences that typically exist between economic and actuarial models of liabilities. The critical step in implementing the methods of Chapter 9 is to define an appropriate model of period-by-period changes in the capital value of fund obligations as a baseline return for each asset. After that, investment policy benchmark optimization is relatively straightforward. The economic liability returns form the basis of the benchmark-relative optimization parameter inputs and computation of efficient frontier portfolios.

ENDOWMENT FUND INVESTMENT POLICY

An endowment fund's investment objective is sometimes defined as maintaining purchasing power over time. Meeting the inflation rate is a simple and convenient interpretation of the fund's obligations. In this case, the historical inflation rate may be the benchmark-relative liability return in each period.[5] An often more thoughtful alternative is to define the fund's obligations in terms of maintaining a college's competitiveness

---

5. Maintaining purchasing power over time is often useful for defining funding liabilities for many financial intermediaries.

among schools of similar character with respect to attracting students and teachers. For example, a given fund may serve as a vehicle for financing student aid. For this fund, an appropriate economic liability model of benchmark return may include historic changes in student costs, including tuition, fees, and living expenses. The size of the fund and the needs of the school relative to competitors are also important considerations.

PENSION LIABILITIES AND BENCHMARK OPTIMIZATION

For many fund trustees and consultants, pension plan liabilities are inextricably associated with actuarial estimation methods. To the extent that economic liability benchmark optimization is a universal framework for defining investment policy, it must be applicable to defined benefit (DB) pension plans. The rest of this chapter explains how benchmark-relative optimization with economic liability modeling can be applied to defining investment policy for DB pension plans. In the process, the economic nature of DB pension plan liabilities is addressed, a topic of substantial interest to many investors. Some limitations of actuarial methods for defining investment policy are also covered.

LIMITATIONS OF ACTUARIAL LIABILITY ESTIMATION

The reader may be surprised to know that pension liability estimation is not the primary focus of DB pension plan actuarial estimation. Instead, the objective of the process is to estimate required plan contributions for the orderly funding of current and emerging plan obligations over time. In many cases, the DB plan corporate funding objective is to maintain pension costs as a fixed percentage, such as 3%, of payroll. Actuarial pension liabilities are simply constructs within the actuarial process for estimating plan contributions.

Many actuarial assumptions are economically unrealistic. Actuarial pension liabilities can be made larger or smaller depending on corporate funding needs and objectives, including whether the corporation prefers to pay benefits now or later. Misperceptions of liability risk, including the illusion of minimal period-by-period variability, are associated with the smoothing methods intrinsic to the actuarial estimation process and the tradition of occasional in-depth actuarial valuations. Misperceptions of liability risk resulting from the actuarial valuation process by financial analysts are responsible for many abuses associated with plan funding and are a primary factor in the demise of many DB pension plans.

For financial planning purposes, actuarial methods may be useful primarily for approximating the current capital value of plan benefits and funding status. Current funding status may be important for defining investment policy, particularly when plan underfunding is significant and plan termination is a serious consideration. Actuarial methods have severe limitations for reflecting pension liability risk.

Economic pension liability models depend on an understanding of the economic nature of pension plan obligations, particularly their role in maintaining corporate competitiveness. The variability of pension liabilities depends primarily on economic factors that are largely outside the scope of actuarial methods. A key to understanding the risks of pension liabilities is to recognize that there are two types of pension liabilities: current or accrued and future or expected. For defining investment policy, pension liability risk dominates the investment policy decision.

CURRENT PENSION LIABILITIES

Plan termination obligations are a first-order consideration for many plan sponsors. This is because plan termination is often a significant corporate consideration, particularly if the firm is in financial distress. Under U.S. law, vested pension benefits are financial obligations of the plan and of the firm, whether or not the plan terminates. The accrued benefit obligation (ABO) defines the capital value at market interest rates associated with plan termination benefits.

Plan termination liabilities are associated with retirees and the vested benefits of current employees. Assume a current employee with 10 years of vested service and 10 years to retirement. If plan termination occurs, the plan has the financial obligation to pay the accumulated plan benefits associated with 10 years of service and current final average salary 10 years from now. The promised benefit in this case is similar to a long-term bond with a delayed first payment period. The plan benefits for retirees have no delay in payment period. The benefit payments of accrued or current plan obligations under plan termination are highly predictable cash flows derivable from mortality tables. Such liabilities are primarily interest rate sensitive and financially similar to a portfolio of short- and long-term bonds.

TOTAL AND VARIABLE PENSION LIABILITIES

Suppose that the firm is ongoing and plan termination is not a significant consideration. In this case, there are additional plan liabilities. Consider again the vested employee with 10 years of service and 10 years until retirement. Suppose that the employee remains with the firm until retirement. In this case the employee's 10 years of current service is associated with a pension benefit that depends on final average pay 10 years from now. The capital value of a benefit that depends on final average pay 10 years from now is likely to be significantly greater than the plan benefit evaluated with current final average pay. Consequently, the value of funds that are required to consider the plan fully funded for all the promised benefits, current and likely, may be much larger than that associated with plan termination. Because the purpose of the pension fund is to assist the firm in providing orderly funding of plan benefits, proper planning includes estimation of expected or emerging benefits associated with the ongoing functioning of the plan. The capital value of the difference between termination and total liabilities may be significant, especially for senior officers of the firm.

Define the estimated capital value at a given point in time of all current and expected plan benefits as the total benefit obligation (TBO) of the pension plan. It is convenient to define the variable benefit obligation (VBO) of the pension plan as the difference between the TBO and ABO:

$$VBO = TBO - ABO.$$

The VBO is the expected pension benefit component of total pension liability. Estimates of required funding levels and considerations of the risk characteristics of pension obligations often ignore the VBO.

ECONOMIC SIGNIFICANCE OF VARIABLE LIABILITIES

Is the VBO a significant portion of the total pension obligation? For companies in mature industries, the VBO may be a relatively minor portion of total plan obligations. This is because most pension obligations may be associated with employees near or at retirement. On the other hand, for fast-growing companies, the VBO may be the dominant portion of plan liabilities. One estimate is that the VBO is typically 70% of the ABO (Michaud, 1989c).

A plan sponsor has the option of terminating the pension plan. Does this make VBO liabilities unimportant? In plan termination, the VBO has zero capital value by definition, and the TBO equals the ABO. Consequently, the view may be that only assets for funding ABO liabilities are required. Such arguments ignore some fundamental economic truths.

By definition, a pension plan is deferred wages. The pension plan is part of the total wage and fringe benefit package associated with employment at the firm. Terminating the pension plan implies a reduction in total compensation paid by the firm to its employees. A firm that terminates the plan and wants to remain in business will have to be competitive for human capital. In equilibrium, this means that the firm has to pay equivalent capital value of terminated benefits either in current wages or some alternative employee benefit. Consequently, there is no economic benefit to the firm purely from plan termination.

In practice firms terminate their DB pension plan and replace it with a defined contribution (DC) pension benefit. One reason for doing so is that DC plans are less expensive. However, the firm may also have to deal with poor employee morale if perceptions of significant diminished total compensation are prevalent. A significant economic disadvantage attaches to plan termination for the ongoing firm. Up to a limit defined by U.S. law, plan contributions are tax advantaged. By terminating the plan the firm may give up an economic benefit that may cost significantly more than its equivalent capital value in total compensation to employees.

Plan termination makes economic sense primarily in the context of substantial financial distress or significant concern for the firm's viability. In this case, the economic value of terminating the plan may be worth the likely near-term decrease in competitiveness for human capital or longer-term increase in total compensation required. For a competitive ongoing firm, the VBO is very much an economic reality, whether or not the plan terminates. Proper investment policy planning requires consideration of both components of total plan liabilities. Contrary to popular perceptions, in the light of tax implications, a DB pension plan is not a corporate liability but a U.S. government-sponsored asset for promoting corporate competitiveness.

ECONOMIC CHARACTERISTICS OF VBO LIABILITIES

The economic risk characteristics of VBO liabilities are generally very different from the ABO. ABO liabilities have fixed-income risk characteristics that are highly sensitive to interest rates. In contrast, VBO liabilities may often have equity risk characteristics and may not be particularly interest rate sensitive (Michaud, 1989b). These fundamental differences have important implications for defining an appropriate DB pension plan investment policy.

VBO risk is associated with the business risks of the firm and its ability to grow and compete for markets and human capital over time. Unexpected changes in VBO liabilities and the firm's payroll are closely associated. Unexpected economic factors that positively affect firm growth are likely to lead to a lower withdrawal rate, larger-than-anticipated salary increases, and unanticipated increases in the workforce, leading to an unexpected increase in firm payroll and VBO liability. Conversely, unexpected economic factors that adversely affect firm growth are likely to have the opposite impact on withdrawal rates and salary and workforce growth, leading to an unexpected decrease in payroll and VBO liability. Consequently, VBO risk is closely linked to regional, national, and global economic risk factors. In some cases, VBO risk may be highly correlated with domestic and global equity market returns and largely unrelated to interest rate risk.[6]

The implications of modeling pension liability risk with economic risk factors can have a dramatic impact on defining investment policy. For example, a VBO with equity risk characteristics may imply that a well-diversified equity portfolio is the low-risk asset allocation of choice, a significant inversion of many conventional perceptions.[7] Local and global

---

6. Michaud (1989b) provides an example.
7. Note that this conclusion is impossible with actuarial liability methods, where the rationalization for equities rests on presumed long-term return benefits as opposed to period-by-period risk characteristics. The example provides further illustration of critical limitations of actuarial methods and standard asset and liability management (ALM) frameworks for defining investment policy.

economic risk factors that affect variable liabilities are often very different from those that affect fixed cash flow securities.

AN EXAMPLE: ECONOMIC LIABILITY PENSION INVESTMENT POLICY

Defining investment policy for a DB pension plan typically involves extensive investigation into the nature of the firm's business risks, the level of current plan liabilities, and the thoughtful use of historic asset returns and economic data. The following discussion provides a very simple example of the benchmark-relative economic liability optimization framework for defining DB pension plan investment policy.

Suppose that the total pension plan liability consists of 60% ABO and 40% VBO and that the plan is fully funded.[8] Also, assume that U.S. bond returns model the ABO, and U.S. equity returns model the VBO. Finally, suppose that the historic period and asset return data of the base case in Tables 2.3 and 2.4 reflect an appropriate scenario for examining investment policy.

According to a 60% bond and 40% equity liability model, Euro and U.S. bonds as well as Canadian equities have a negative benchmark-relative return for the base case data. Referring to the index-relative discussion in

Table 10.1 Benchmark-Relative Constraint Priors

	Euro Bonds	US Bonds	Canada	France	Germany	Japan	UK	US
Min	0%	0%	0%	0%	0%	0%	0%	40%
Max	0%	60%	0%	100%	100%	100%	100%	100%

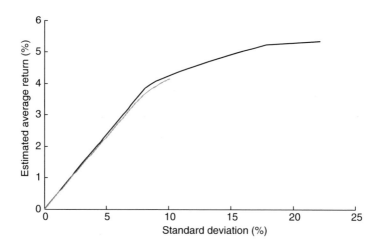

Exhibit 10.1 Liability-Relative MV and RE Frontiers

8. Full funding here means that the capital value of the fund equals the TBO. See Michaud (1989c) for benchmark optimization under more general funding assumptions.

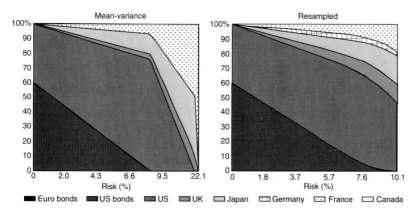

Exhibit 10.2 Liability-Relative MV and RE Optimal Composition Maps

Chapter 9 and Table 9.2, the RE optimization constraint priors associated with a 40/60 U.S. stock/bond benchmark are given in Table 10.1.

Exhibit 10.1 compares the liability-relative MV efficient portfolios to RE optimized portfolios with Table 10.1 constraint priors. The left-hand panel of Exhibit 10.2 provides the MV liability-relative efficient frontier composition map; the right-hand panel displays the RE liability-relative Table 10.1 constraint priors composition map. In-sample, the MV efficient frontier portfolios reflect higher potential of return and wider range of risk than the REF. The composition maps reflect a very different view of liability-relative portfolio optimality.

Exhibit 10.3 provides the results on average of investment period simulation performance associated with a liability-relative truth represented by the MV efficient frontier in Exhibit 10.1. The results show that the out-of-sample performance of the RE optimal liability-relative constraint prior optimized portfolios outperforms their associated liability-relative

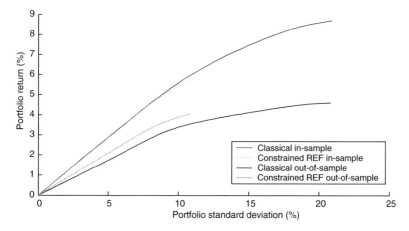

Exhibit 10.3 Liability-Relative MV and RE Performance

MV optimized portfolios by a wide margin. RE optimization, properly implemented, has the potential for dramatic improvement of optimized portfolio performance as well as redefining liability-relative optimality.

PAST AND FUTURE OF DEFINED BENEFIT PENSION PLANS

DB pension plans are rapidly disappearing and being converted to DC pension plans. DC plans imply lower contributions for the firm as well as transfer responsibility of fund investment performance to employees and retirees. Given the need to be competitive globally, a DC plan may be a competitive necessity for many firms. Employees are disadvantaged in that DC plans are unlikely to provide similar DB plan benefit levels, nor will they be able to rely on any specific level of benefits of lifetime income and legacies. However, employees find DC plans desirable because benefits are portable. Few employees expect lifetime employment from corporations today. Plan terminations often occur in mergers and acquisitions. Funding inadequacies that lead to distress plan terminations by the Pension Benefit Guarantee Corporation (PBGC) typically result in a fraction of promised benefits to plan participants. For many, 50% of something is preferable to 100% of nothing.

The objective of the 2006 Pension Protection Act (PPA) is to provide more incentives for maintaining adequate funding of DB pension plans. However, many consider the act too little too late. The likely demise of most DB pension plans due to funding inadequacies is unfortunate since many participants would be better off covered by responsible management of a DB pension plan in retirement. Funding inadequacies can often be traced to two common errors that were in many cases avoidable: deviations from planned actuarial contributions and exotic investment management. The actuarial estimation process assumes a fixed percentage of payroll for funding across the lifetime of the fund. Given reasonable functioning of capital markets and firm viability, corporate funding at the assumed actuarial rate was often likely to meet short- and long-term needs of the plan for the life of the firm. It was also a sensible way to plan for pension expense. Note that a fixed percentage of payroll contribution policy is designed to manage the VBO as well as ABO of the plan over the lifetime of the fund. Under the actuarial assumptions, a conventional stock/bond asset mix of diversified low-cost domestic and international stocks and bonds with risk level optimized with respect to the business risks of the firm and maturity of the workforce would have been likely to adequately fund the plan. Attempts to improve investment performance typically included more risky investments that added unnecessary volatility in many cases to pension funding.

Prior to the 1974 Employees Retirement Income Security Act (ERISA), pension benefits relied on the goodwill of the corporation. Pension plans were often administered as a part-time activity by relatively low-level corporate officers. Plan termination bore little economic disincentive apart from declining employee morale and productivity. ERISA transformed pension benefits into a tax lien of the firm with required contributions. Pension trustees were now responsible for real commitments and costs. Pension expense had to be managed as any other expense of the firm.

With ERISA, corporate contributions were mandated expenses that could affect earnings and stock valuation. Under the guise of investment efficiency, investment banks and pension consultants courted pension plan trustees with various generally riskier investment strategies with the goal of pension cost reduction. The critical link between payroll and pension costs was severed. Due to the large sums of money often involved, pension trustees became Wall Street celebrities and in turn were often courted by finance and entertainment celebrities. Introducing sophisticated investment strategies (with attendant legal and Wall Street fees) promised lower contributions and better firm earnings that enhanced the importance of plan trustees in the corporation. Funding holidays were seen as desirable goals. Various termination strategies were promoted as ways of making the corporation more globally competitive. Unions demanding benefit improvements whenever the fortunes of the plan turned unexpectedly positive served to reinforce the sense that thoughtful pension administration was self-defeating. Unions were unlikely to propose rolling back benefit improvements when the plan was in distress.

DB plans have borne much abuse by many involved in plan funding management. Patriarchal management is no longer fashionable in American corporate culture. Firms need to be globally competitive in ways that were unnecessary in earlier times. As a consequence, a DC pension plan is likely to be the retirement benefit framework of choice for most corporations and employees in the future. Some important factors are emerging to support the viability of DC plans for participants. These include enhanced access to professional asset management and improved availability of institutional-quality retirement planning tools. American firms and their employees may ultimately be better off leaving responsibility for pension benefits to employees customized to lifestyle needs and objectives.

CONCLUSION

Economic liability-relative RE optimization, performed appropriately, is often a significant tool for enhancing the value of investment policy studies. In spite of its simplicity, the example indicates that a benchmark-relative RE optimized economic liability framework may substantially enhance the investment value of MV optimization.

As a practical matter, economic liability risk modeling may not be a simple process. Most critically, it may often require abandoning basic misconceptions of funding and plan liability risk. The key to the success of the procedure is to define a relevant and appropriate economic liability model of total fund liabilities. On the positive side, fund trustees and corporate officers often find an economic liability approach to investment policy planning an attractive and institutionally meaningful process.

Many applications of economic liability modeling remain to be developed. Many issues are open, and extensive research is required to solve specific applications.

11

Bayes and Active Return Estimation

Active asset managers have views of the returns and risks of assets and capital markets that are an integral part of their investment process. Risk-return estimates in a portfolio optimization are typically a combination of current and historical information. Active equity management depends on estimates of alpha—risk-adjusted excess return relative to a benchmark index—that reflect the expertise, strategy, market outlook, and resources of the firm. Tactical asset allocation managers employ a variety of methods to estimate market and asset returns. Strategic or long-term asset allocators use historic return data informed with current information to develop strategies and policies. By adding exogenous views, investment managers act as Bayesian agents improving the forecast value of historically estimated optimization inputs.

While asset managers are natural Bayesians, few use formal Bayesian procedures for including views in optimization estimates. Typically, exogenous views simply replace some or all of historically estimated inputs. This chapter presents a simple yet effective and rigorous framework for integrating exogenous estimates of returns in portfolio optimization inputs. A properly used Bayesian framework has the potential to significantly improve the investment value of optimized portfolios in practice. Bayesian estimates provide a useful framework to further explore the relative importance of enhanced optimization versus enhanced risk-return estimates in optimized portfolio performance.

CURRENT PRACTICES

Historic return data similar to those described in Chapter 2 are often the starting point for risk-return estimates in an asset allocation.[1] However, in actual practice, managers often replace historical average returns with exogenous estimates based on current views of markets and assets. This is because they view historically estimated returns as generally unreliable. Similarly, equity portfolio managers typically use a commercial equity risk measurement service to estimate the components of portfolio risk and employ a separate process for estimating return or alpha.

The practice of disconnecting return from risk estimation has important investment limitations. Ad hoc return estimates are often inconsistent with historic asset variability and interrelationships represented by estimated correlations. In addition, simply replacing historic average returns with ad hoc returns ignores the reliability of exogenous estimates.[2]

BAYES PRINCIPLES

A Bayes procedure is essentially a conditional probability statement. To illustrate, in a deck of playing cards the probability of randomly choosing a heart is one fourth. However, if we happen to know that the card drawn is a red card, the additional information improves the probability of choosing a heart to one half. In the same way, reliable exogenous investment information not reflected in historic data may be used to increase the accuracy of risk-return estimates. A Bayes procedure is designed to summarize probabilistically two independent sources of information relative to one future event.

THE BAYES RETURN FORMULA

A formula for computing a Bayes estimate for return is given in (11.1). In the formula the mean returns are vectors and variances are covariance matrices:[3]

$$\text{Bayes Mean} = B\mu + (I - B)\,y \qquad (11.1)$$

---

1. Statistical procedures that enhance the investment value of the historic data, such as the Stein methods in Chapter 8, may be part of the process.
2. This disconnect exists widely in equity portfolio optimization practice, where alpha is an internal estimation process while risk comes from a commercial service. However, in the equity optimization case, a Bayesian process that connects risk and return in an integrated framework has many challenges. Risk estimation is a serious data management problem. In addition, the components of risk are not always investment return intuitive. Equity alpha estimation is in itself a very difficult problem. The technology for integrating risk and return for large stock indices remains an elusive ideal for many institutions. At the current state of asset management technology, Bayes estimation may be most relevant for asset allocation and stock alpha estimation.
3. Carlin and Louis (1992, p. 22). The formula assumes multivariate normal distributions.

Where
  μ = historic estimated mean returns
  y = exogenous estimates views
  Σ_h = historic return estimated covariances
  Σ_v = exogenous views covariances[4]
  I = identity matrix
  $B = \Sigma_h^{-1}(\Sigma_h^{-1} + \Sigma_v^{-1})^{-1}$

The formula is simple to interpret. The Bayes or mixed mean estimate (11.1) of return represents a weighted average of what we observe (μ) and what we forecast (y). It is weighted by the percentage of the total variance B explained by the historic data.

This formula is a simple generalization of Theil and Goldberger (1961).[5] In our formulation of the Bayes mean, you need use only the views of any asset you have at the level of certainty you have. This Bayes formula allows for Stein estimation or other statistical procedures for refining the forecast value of historically estimated data. It allows for linear constrained MV and RE optimization for any choice of risk along the frontier.[6]

There are many sources of information and methods that asset managers may use to develop views for input into a Bayesian mean mixed estimation process. These include empirical and theoretical principles of finance, current business and economic data, recent regulatory and political and socioeconomic events, and various econometric forecasting methods. Indeed, a Bayesian estimation process defines a Bayes panel that can comprehensively represent the firm's investment process at a particular moment.

A BAYES PANEL ILLUSTRATION

To illustrate the Bayes return estimation process, assume investment committee estimates of future return at 9% for France and 8% for Japan. The committee associates a level of certainty or range of variation (standard deviation) of 15% for its estimates. The committee expresses no other views apart from those given by the historic data. A lack of an exogenous view for an asset is indicated by a certainty level (standard deviation) of 999%.

---

4. The variances or diagonal elements in Σ_v reflect the level of reliability of the exogenous return estimates. The off-diagonal elements are covariances that are often based on historically estimated correlations due to the difficulty of reliable exogenous estimation.
5. See Theil (1971) for an authoritative and comprehensive discussion.
6. The Bayes formula (11.1) is the same as used in Black and Litterman (1992). However, the implementation of the formula in the text is free of the restricting assumptions in Black-Litterman. Their framework—unbounded MV optimization—inherits the Jobson and Korkie out-of-sample performance limitations and is unsuitable for linear-constrained MV and RE optimization. In addition, the procedure requires identification of the equilibrium market portfolio and risk premium, which is unnecessary in our formulation.

Table 11.1 Bayes Panel for Estimating Return

Asset Names	Historic Data		Views		Bayes Results
	Avg Return	Std Dev	Return	Certainty	
Euro Bonds	3.2%	5.4%	0.0%	999.0%	3.1%
US Bonds	3.0%	7.0%	0.0%	999.0%	2.9%
Canada	4.6%	19.0%	0.0%	999.0%	4.1%
France	10.5%	24.4%	9.0%	15.0%	9.3%
Germany	6.4%	21.5%	0.0%	999.0%	5.5%
Japan	10.5%	24.4%	8.0%	15.0%	8.6%
UK	9.5%	20.8%	0.0%	999.0%	8.7%
US	8.5%	14.9%	0.0%	999.0%	8.2%

Table 11.1 displays the Bayes return estimates from formula (11.1) given our assumptions. Columns 2 and 3 repeat the CPI-adjusted annualized average returns and standard deviations for the base case data in Tables 2.3 and 2.4 for the indicated assets. Column 4 displays the future return views for France and Japan and column 5 the associated level of certainty. Column 6 provides the formula (11.1) Bayesian mixed estimate return for each asset class.

Reviewing the results in Table 11.1, it is not surprising to see that the Bayesian estimates for France and Japan are lower and closer to the committee's views than the historically estimated returns. What is interesting is how the returns of the other assets react to the new information. While the returns are all lower than historic, some are much lower than others on a relative basis. Apart from the bonds, the U.S. is little affected by the committee's lower return estimate for global assets. This is because the U.S. market is least correlated with Europe and Japan.

The RE optimized portfolios change as well with the new rates of return. Exhibit 11.1 presents the composition map of the RE optimized portfolios constructed with the Bayes estimates of return in Table 11.1. Compare the portfolios to the RE composition map in Exhibit 6.3. As risk increases, the changes in the return estimates become more prominent. In particular, using the Bayes estimates dictates that Japan has a less dominant role while U.S. equities have a larger one.

BAYESIAN MIXED ESTIMATION ISSUES

The hallmark of the Bayes procedure presented here is flexibility. Reliability levels provide the investment committee with a great deal of control of the results, from reflecting largely the historic-based return estimates to largely the return forecasts. The analyst soon comes to appreciate the interaction of reliability level and historic interrelationships for designing

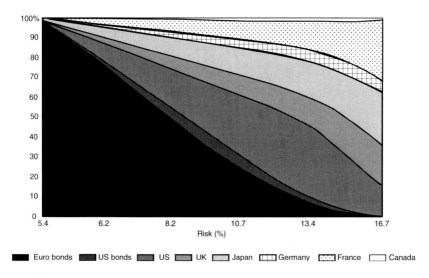

Exhibit 11.1 RE Optimal Composition Map, Bayes Panel Return Estimates

the optimization inputs and obtaining maximum benefit from the forecasts consistent with beliefs.

The reader may find the asset allocation mixed estimation results in
Table 11.1 obvious and largely anticipatable. However, the process is often
a world away from the ad hoc return procedures and resulting MV asset
allocations prevalent in the investment community today. The results in
Exhibit 11.1 do not differ drastically from the original efficient frontier
in spite of the influence of the forecasts, in no small measure due to the
stability of the RE optimization process. In contrast, ad hoc procedures
for developing return forecasts often lead to dramatically different clas-
sically optimized portfolios. Mixed estimation with RE optimization is
likely to have a first-order impact on the stability and investment benefit
of optimized asset allocations.[7]

Why do so few managers use a rigorous Bayesian estimation framework? The difficulties emerge when attempting to implement the process
in actual practice.

In the Bayesian framework of (11.1), exogenous views are assumed
independent of historically estimated data. In practice, the independence
requirement is difficult to satisfy. Manager views are often strongly influ-
enced by recent market and economic history. In addition, the reliability
of the manager's views must be determined in some way. Also, a Bayesian framework does not eliminate the need for conditioning historic
return data appropriately or estimating risk.

7. It should not be surprising to note that more complex formulas also exist.

Properly understood, the Bayes panel in Exhibit 11.1 emerges as nothing less than a complete, rigorous description of a professional
manager's investment process. Various investment strategies and investment mandates can be accommodated within the context of a Bayes
panel. Consequently, the level of difficulty associated with a Bayes panel
is no more than a reflection of the demands of a rigorous framework for
codifying an investment strategy.

A cautionary note: Although the mixed estimation process is very
flexible, it is also prone to user error. Successful implementation often
requires experience and patience with the procedure as well as significant attention to detail.

ENHANCED INPUTS OR ENHANCED OPTIMIZER

Asset managers typically devote a great deal of their resources to improving risk-return estimates in an effort to improve optimized portfolio performance. As previously shown, RE optimization is another route for
improved portfolio performance. Is improved estimation more important
than improved optimization?

Markowitz and Usmen (2003) address the issue of the relative importance of improved inputs and classical efficiency versus RE optimization.
They develop a sophisticated diffuse Bayesian procedure to enhance
risk-return estimation. Using the simulation test framework laid out in
Chapter 6, they compare the performance of their Bayes-enhanced risk-
return estimates with MV optimization to RE optimization with unenhanced
risk-return estimates. They were surprised to find that the RE optimized
portfolios without Bayesian enhanced risk-return estimates exhibited superior performance on average and in every one of their 30 individual tests.

A replication of the Markowitz-Usmen test using James-Stein estimation as a substitute for their more sophisticated Bayesian procedure found
similar results. Exhibit 11.2 displays the indicated in-sample (dotted) and
out-of-sample (solid) MV and RE frontiers from the simulation test. For
reference, the "true" MV efficient frontier is the middle solid frontier and
in-sample MV efficiency without James-Stein is plotted as the top dotted curve. The in-sample James-Stein MV efficient frontier has been cali-
brated to provide a useful estimate of the true MV efficient frontier.[8]

The in-sample MV efficient frontier with James-Stein estimation is
much closer to the true MV efficient frontier than the frontier without
James-Stein. This result is consistent with expectations and contrasts with
the relatively poor estimate of the true MV frontier by the in-sample REF.

8. All simulations in Exhibit 11.2 are based on 10 years of monthly simulated (120) returns from Michaud
(1998) risk-return estimates. The number of simulated returns was used to provide a good estimate of
the James-Stein MV efficient frontier estimate relative to the true efficient frontier. The results also use
the Ledoit (1997) estimate of the covariance matrix. Eighteen years of simulated monthly returns used
in other studies in this report would not have provided a good James-Stein MV frontier estimate.

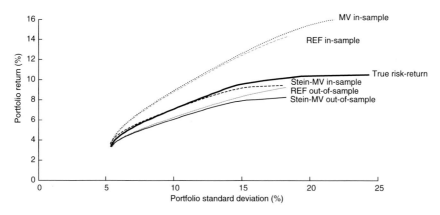

Exhibit 11.2 RE versus Stein-MV Optimized Performance

However, consistent with Markowitz and Usmen (2003), unenhanced estimated REF dominates out-of-sample performance. Superior optimization dominates superior estimation in the investment period.

The dramatic Markowitz-Usmen results and those of Exhibit 11.2 may appear to defy investment intuition but in fact are easy to explain. MV optimization always assumes unrealistic accuracy of investment information (16 decimal places) independent of the quality of the estimates. This level of accuracy is inconsistent with information in investment practice. As a result, classical optimization always overuses investment information and creates extreme portfolios that typically perform poorly in practice whatever the quality of the information. Harvey et al. (2003) characterize the Michaud optimization resampling approach as changing the order of Bayesian integration. The Markowitz-Usmen and our results indicate that order of integration may be nontrivially important.

BAYESIAN CAVEATS

Formal Bayesian methodologies have an important limitation. Bayesian estimation is not always a better procedure; a perverse prior may lead to poorer, not better, estimates. Avoiding a perverse prior is the reason why Markowitz and Usmen (2003) use a diffuse prior in their estimation process.[9] The perverse Bayes prior problem is a major concern in statistical estimation theory. Efron (2005), in his American Statistical Association presidential address, advocates "empirical Bayes" methods to avoid

9. Harvey et al. (2003) claim to improve on the Markowitz/Usmen/Bayes estimation procedure by including higher moments. Their results, however, are not in the Levy-Markowitz (1979) framework assumed in this book or used by most practitioners. Moreover, they note that their results are aimed at improved in-sample expected utility rather than out-of-sample risk-adjusted performance, as in Markowitz-Usmen and Chapter 6 of this book. While we do not dispute their in-sample results, our focus is on out-of-sample investment performance.

the effects of a perverse prior in Bayesian analysis while attempting to retain its improvement of statistical estimation power. The resampling and bootstrap methods Efron advocates conceptually resemble RE optimization. Given that there is always some uncertainty of risk and return estimates, properly managed, RE optimization is always a recommendable procedure for improving performance on average.

While it is interesting to compare the relative value of statistically improved inputs versus RE optimization, the procedures may be complementary rather than exclusive. Procedures for improving the forecast value of estimates are often worthwhile. Bayesian methods consistent with financial priors can often be recommended for improving RE optimization.

12

Avoiding Optimization Errors

Optimizers are useful for assigning airport gates, computing lunar-trajectories, and routing telephone calls, as well as optimizing portfolios. Therefore, it should not be surprising that an optimizer requires a great deal of information specific to the investment process if it is going to find investment-relevant portfolios. The operating principle for defining an optimization is that more information is better than less as long as it is reliable and consistent.

Several procedures, developed largely from institutional experience, are useful for enhancing the investment value of an optimization. Most apply to equity portfolio optimization.

SCALING INPUTS

Improperly scaled inputs are a major source of errors made in formulating an optimization. In an equity portfolio optimization, there are three basic classes of security inputs: expected returns, trading costs, and risk estimates. In the many cases when the input units are not comparable, optimization results are unlikely to have investment value.

Institutional forecasts of stock returns are generally relative valuations or rankings of stock values.[1] Relative valuations need scaling in order to be useful as inputs to most optimizers. The appropriate scaling

---

1. Forecasts of expected returns might be relative valuations even when they resemble actual returns. For example, Michaud and Davis (1982) show that dividend discount model returns may only have ordinal or stock ranking information.

transforms the return forecast into the "return on average associated with the forecast." Proper scaling of return forecasts allows comparability with trading costs, risk estimates, and other inputs in the optimization.[2]

The scaling formula is the product of two quantities:

1. The assumed level of information or correlation between the forecast and ex post return
2. The expected volatility or standard deviation of ex post returns.

The first quantity is the information correlation or coefficient (IC) of the forecast. The IC and expected volatility may vary by market, sector, industry, and analyst.

The scaling formula for forecast returns has an important subtlety that has often led to error. In many cases, the two components of the scaling formula are inversely related. For example, the IC of a forecast for utility stocks may be higher than for growth stocks, but the level of ex ante volatility may be less. Consequently, the product or scale factor for utility stock forecasts may not differ significantly from that for growth stocks.

Although stock return forecasts are often given in monthly return units, some commercial risk estimate services are provided in weekly units. Inconsistent risk and return units may have a negative impact on the optimization. In some commercial optimizers, the optimized portfolio depends on the values of the parameters of a quadratic "utility" or "risk aversion" function.[3] In this case, the units of the returns and risk estimates affect the solution. However, most commercial services also include an option to define optimality in terms of tracking error. Tracking error-defined optimality is less problematic because it allows the user to ignore risk model units.[4]

The manager must also properly scale expected returns relative to trading cost estimates.[5] Trading costs generally vary by market, holding

---

2. Ambachtsheer (1977) pioneered the development of the scaling formula for forecast returns. Michaud (1989a, appendix, pp. 40–41) generalized the scaling process and developed some of its properties using a linear regression framework. In some cases, a more general regression framework may be appropriate.

3. An optimizer may define a single optimal portfolio on the efficient frontier based on preset values of quadratic "utility function" parameters that define the relative importance of portfolio risk and expected return. One problem is that the choice of default values of the utility parameters may not be appropriate for a given investor. Another problem is that the parameters may have little intuitive investment meaning. In addition, the default values may obscure limitations of the optimizer or risk model. For example, default parameters may be set to choose efficient portfolios near the top of the efficient frontier. The optimizer, in this case, may do little more than find large expected return portfolios. Often, a more meaningful objective is to define an optimal portfolio in terms of the desired level of risk. For optimizers defined by utility function parameters, the manager can compute efficient portfolios with desired risk levels by varying parameter values.

4. By allowing the specification of portfolio residual risk directly, a properly formulated stock portfolio optimizer operates independently of the scaling of the risk estimates relative to the return inputs and trading costs.

5. The three components of total trading costs are fees (including taxes), market impact, and opportunity. The careful estimation of all three components of trading costs is a critical element in the likely investment success of a portfolio optimization.

period, investment style, and asset class. For example, a value strategy may have a much lower portfolio turnover rate than a growth stock strategy. In this case, the average turnover rate may affect the relative scaling of return forecasts to trading costs.

Although the effort may be significant, proper scaling of all optimization inputs is essential. Poorly scaled optimizations usually generate investment-irrelevant optimized portfolios.

FINANCIAL REALITY

It seems obvious to insist that optimization inputs are consistent with financial reality, yet in many cases optimization inputs do not make investment sense.

A surprisingly common error concerns active return or alpha forecasts. By definition, the index-weighted sum of active returns must equal zero; in investment terms, an index can never beat itself. Yet institutional active returns often do not satisfy this necessary condition. Consequently, the optimization may have little investment value. Note that the index-weighted sum constraint is often useful for conditioning historic regressions for forecasting returns.

LIQUIDITY FACTORS

For a large trust department or mutual fund portfolio, or for a small-capitalization stock portfolio, the capital value of the fund may be significant in terms of the percentage of a security's outstanding market value. For example, a 1% change in a holding may represent a large amount of capital relative to the size of the firm. Such considerations are related to trading cost, where the trading cost function depends on portfolio size and is nonlinear. This is an example of the inherent position-dependent character of portfolio optimization.

A related issue is liquidity and capitalization in asset allocation. Country equity and fixed income markets may differ significantly in size and liquidity. An MV asset allocation that does not consider relative liquidity and size may lead to irrelevant portfolios. Some methods for considering such factors include nonlinear trading cost or quadratic constraints.

An implementation liquidity issue has to do with optimized "nuisance" portfolio weights. Conceptually, an RE optimized portfolio has a non-zero weight for all assets in the universe. While consistent with financial theory, in practice many assets may have economically uninvestable allocations. Investability depends on many factors, including the character of information and the state of the market. Three conditions are useful for transforming an optimal portfolio into an investable one: cardinality, threshold, and increments. Cardinality defines the number of assets desired in the investable portfolio. Threshold defines the minimum size portfolio weight desirable for investment. Increment defines an additive unit for investment. The authors have found post optimization of RE optimized portfolios with mixed integer best approximation technology very helpful in defining investable portfolios.

PRACTICAL CONSTRAINT ISSUES

Institutional portfolio optimizations often include many kinds of constraints. Sector and industry membership constraints are a simple way to control portfolio risk. Constraints may reflect investment strategy or market outlook information that is exogenous to return forecasts. Constraints may be useful for imposing quality controls on the portfolio management process. Constraints are also useful for controlling portfolio structure and avoiding inadvertent risk exposures. When no information is available, it is often useful to keep factor and group exposures close to index weights. The downside of portfolio constraints is that they can lead to significant opportunity costs on investment performance if not properly used. Overconstrained portfolios may be substantially riskier out-of-sample than they appear.[6]

The large number of constraints in many institutional portfolio optimizations has evolved from hard-earned investment experience. Investment practice may often reflect the historic need to overcome the many limitations of current MV portfolio optimizers and equity risk models. However, an informed statistical view of portfolio optimization may reduce the need for many constraints and the opportunity costs and risks associated with overconstrained portfolios.

BIASED PORTFOLIO CHARACTERISTICS

As a general principle, any optimized portfolio characteristic is biased because estimation error accumulates in the optimization objective function. One important example is that the risk of an optimized portfolio is a downward-biased estimate of its true value. This means that the out-of-sample risk of an optimized portfolio is likely to be larger than that estimated by the risk model and the optimization. One method of evaluating the unbiased risk of an optimized portfolio is to subscribe to two competent risk measurement services. The recommended procedure is to optimize the portfolio with one risk model and evaluate portfolio risk with the other. Although it is not foolproof, the two-risk measurement method can help to realistically estimate out-of-sample portfolio risk.

The same bias is present for any other optimized portfolio characteristic. For example, a manager may want to maximize dividend yield or minimize portfolio beta. A maximized dividend yield or minimized beta

6. An overly risk-constrained or factor-constrained portfolio may have much more out-of-sample risk than a less constrained portfolio.

portfolio is likely to have a much smaller dividend yield or larger beta out-of-sample than that estimated in the optimization.

Optimizing more than one variable may create additional biases. For example, beta and dividend yield have a negative correlation. Optimizing correlated variables in the same optimization can create synergistic biases and unpredictable portfolio behavior.

In general, the more demands placed on the optimization, the more likely the out-of-sample performance of the optimized portfolio will disappoint. Such effects are endemic to all optimization processes. To be effective, a user should be aware of an optimizer's inherent limitations in using statistically estimated data and conservative in the demands made of the optimization process. However, it should be noted that RE optimization substantially reduces optimization biases in many cases.

INDEX FUNDS AND OPTIMIZERS

The purpose of an index fund is to track an index. One method for constructing index funds is to use MV optimization. The objective is to minimize the residual or tracking error. Because there are no return estimates, an index fund optimization is significantly more stable than a more typical MV optimization. For this reason, optimization may appear as the tool of choice for constructing index-tracking portfolios. However, because of competitive pressures, manager tolerance for tracking error is generally much smaller than for active portfolios. Even small errors in tracking error estimation can have (and have had) significant negative business consequences.

There are two alternative ways to construct index funds in practice: replication and stratified sampling. *Index replication* is constructing an index-weighted portfolio consisting of all the securities in the index.[7] *Stratification* is a statistical sampling procedure for constructing a representative sample portfolio of securities in the index, usually based on index-weighted representative tiers of sectors of securities in the index. The three procedures differ in comprehensiveness of representation of the index: Replication is the most comprehensive, whereas optimization is usually the least.

Various considerations determine which procedure to choose in a given situation. Minimum tracking error and rebalancing issues may make replication the method of choice for long-term investors. In some cases where the liquidity or holding costs of stocks in an index are a major consideration, optimization or stratified sampling may be more appropriate alternatives. In some emerging markets where a reliable risk model may not be available, stratification may be the procedure of choice.

---

7. In practice, the portfolio may exclude many small stocks.

OPTIMIZATION FROM CASH

The appropriate procedure for optimizing an equity portfolio may depend on whether the optimization starts from cash or from a fully invested equity portfolio (Erlich, 1997). To frame the issue, note that equity portfolios are generally decomposable into two portfolios: an index fund and a pure active or arbitrage portfolio.[8] If we suppose an indefinite holding period for the invested assets, rebalancing may occur many times over the life of the fund.

An active manager optimizes the portfolio according to the active return forecasts. Conceptually, the index is the appropriate starting portfolio. When optimizing from cash, however, the objective of optimally investing in the active or arbitrage portfolio conflicts with the need to convert cash into the index. The active return forecasts are relevant for a single, often relatively short-term, forecast period. Each rebalancing period has different active return forecasts. In contrast, the index component of the fund is relatively stable. Eventually, the cost of converting cash into the stock index is paid. The optimizer has to compromise between the dual objectives of finding an optimal arbitrage portfolio and investing in the stock index portfolio. Rebalancing periods when the purchase of the index fund is incomplete exposes the optimized portfolio to unnecessary and irrelevant risk and trading costs.

A preferable procedure is to invest cash in two optimization steps. First, find an optimal portfolio from cash, omitting active return forecasts, that considers the investor's objectives and constraints, including residual risk target, desired number of securities, and trading cost estimates. This step defines a neutral or index-like portfolio that reflects the normal constraints and objectives that are part of the relatively stable structure of the fund. The second step starts with the neutral portfolio to define an optimal active portfolio as a function of the active return forecasts. The arbitrage component of the active portfolio in the second-step optimization reflects tradeoffs between return forecasts, risk, and trading costs independent of the need to convert cash into equities. Because the cost of buying the neutral portfolio has to be paid, there is no overall increase in trading cost over the normal life of the fund.

The Erlich two-step optimization procedure balances the long-term objective of buying the neutral portfolio with the shorter-term objective of implementing the active return forecasts. The procedure is likely to result in better performance, less risk, more stability during early rebalancings, and a reduction in overall trading costs.

Cash optimization may also be useful when adding cash to an equity portfolio. More generally, two-step optimization may be useful when there is a change in the benchmark portfolio or other long-term

---

8. The weights of the arbitrage portfolio sum to zero, while the index fund weights sum to one. See Michaud (1993) for further discussion.

characteristics of the fund. The importance of two-step optimization may increase as the size of the stock universe and level of active portfolio risk increases. For low-risk and single-country equity portfolios, the benefits may not be significant.

FORECAST RETURN LIMITATIONS

Useful optimized portfolios require careful control of portfolio structure. This is because forecast returns may have implicit structural biases that are not part of the information in the stock valuation process.

Generally, active equity optimization returns are adjusted for systematic risk. However, there are many open theoretical and practical issues with estimating the return associated with systematic risk. For example, Kandel and Stambaugh (1995) note some important limitations of widely used econometric estimation methods. From another perspective, Berk's (1995) theoretical analysis suggests that many systematic risk frameworks may not correctly reflect the risk of small stocks. In addition, the proper theoretical framework for estimating systematic risk remains controversial in some cases.[9]

Another source of biases may come from the structure of the returns. Suppose that the stock forecasts are market sector neutral.[10] For example, a forecast may be based on a factor-return regression that includes sector dummy variables to adjust for sector returns. Nevertheless, the unconstrained optimized portfolio may exhibit large overweights and underweights in various market sectors. If there is no sector information in the return forecast, why are there sector underweights and overweights?

Variables used to forecast return, such as the book-to-price ratio, are likely to have larger-than-average values in some sectors than in others. A larger-than-average value of the forecast factors in a sector is likely to lead to a larger-than-average value of forecast return in the sector. Consequently, all other things the same, the unconstrained optimized portfolio is overweighted in some sectors and underweighted in others. However, by definition of a sector-neutral forecast, there is no sector weighting information in the return.[11] In this case, the structure of returns leads to inadvertent portfolio biases that are not consistent with the sources of information in the forecast. One simple way to eliminate inadvertent biases in optimized portfolios is to impose index weight constraints on factor exposures that do not reflect forecast return information.

---

9. For example, Shanken (1992, 1996) provides critiques of the arbitrage pricing theory framework that is the basis of many commercial models of equity risk measurement.

10. Michaud (1999) provides an example.

11. It should be noted that other formulations of forecast return may have sector-weighting information. The point of the example is to show that inadvertent portfolio bets may appear in an unconstrained optimized portfolio.

Biases in forecast returns may be pervasive and are often very subtle. Analysts and investment managers need to be diligent in detecting and eliminating such biases. Portfolio optimization is likely to fail to provide useful investment portfolios unless the process is well formulated and consistent with risk estimation and the relevant sources of information in the forecasts.

CONCLUSION

Avoiding implementation errors is important for capturing and enhancing the investment value of optimizers. Thoughtful consideration of investment theory and intuition, investor objectives, forecast return biases, and optimizer behavior leads to specialized techniques that may have a significant positive impact on portfolio structure and optimized portfolio performance.

Epilogue

The most serious limitations of MV efficiency as a practical tool of investment management are instability, ambiguity, ineffectiveness, and rigidity. Small input errors lead to large errors in the optimized portfolio. By maximizing the use of statistical errors in parameter estimates, an MV optimized portfolio often has little, if any, investment value. In addition, because of instability, MV efficiency may be ambiguous and poorly defined in practice.

The practical limitations of MV optimization are not a reflection of conceptual flaws in Markowitz MV efficiency but of implementation. Markowitz gives you the right way to invest in many practical cases assuming you have, and know that you have, the correct estimates. But investment information is inherently uncertain. MV optimization ignores the statistical character of investment information. The power of the algorithm is generally far greater than the level of investment information in the inputs. Alternatives to MV efficiency typically have significant practical limitations and do not improve investment effectiveness.

Implementation errors often reflect a lack of understanding of the importance of estimation error and the fundamental statistical nature of portfolio optimization. MV optimization is simply statistical estimation and requires statistical methods and analysis. Although statistical methods have developed naturally in the context of multivariate linear regression, the history of MV efficiency has had a limiting effect on its statistical development until now. Resampling is the procedure of choice for dealing with the statistical character of investment information in linear constrained MV optimized portfolios. Resampled Efficiency methods use the uncertainty implicit in investment information to improve asset management in practice.

Historically, large segments of the institutional investment management community have ignored MV optimization. In hindsight, the reason is simply because MV optimization did not work well enough to add investment value and represented too rigid a framework for sophisticated asset management. Yet the investment community has much at stake in improving Markowitz efficiency. MV optimization properly used is the wide-spectrum engine of choice for sophisticated asset management for many applications in practice.

Much effort remains to improve the investment value of MV optimization. There are many open issues and challenges. An awareness of their importance will, it is hoped, spur funding and research in these areas. However, the fact that the limitations of MV optimization have been ignored for so long raises troubling issues of the state of sophistication of institutional research and investment practice and of academic–professional relationships.[1] Perhaps some lasting lessons can be learned for the future.

1. That much pioneering work on estimation error and the limitations of MV optimization as a practical tool for asset management was ignored for many years has numerous parallels in the history of science. A notable recent example is described in Altman (2005) of Dr. A. Stone Freedberg of Harvard who in 1940 published his findings of the bacterial cause of ulcers and a possible cure. Subsequent flawed research failed to corroborate his findings and closed the publishing door on further work on curing ulcers for more than fifty years. The 2005 Nobel Prize in Medicine was awarded for independently discovering and verifying Dr. Freedberg's results. Science has a strong vested interest in correcting erroneous notions before flawed research takes root and leads researchers away from productive paths.

Bibliography

Alexander, Gordon, and Jack Clark Francis. 1986. *Portfolio Analysis*, 3rd ed. Englewood Cliffs, NJ: Prentice-Hall.

Altman, L. 2005. "A Scientist, Gazing Toward Stockholm, Ponders 'What If?'" *New York Times* 6 December. Science Times: 5.

Ambachtsheer, Keith. 1977. "Where are the Customers' Alphas?" *Journal of Portfolio Management* 4(1): 52–56.

Barry, C. B. 1974. "Portfolio Analysis Under Uncertain Means." *Journal of Finance,* 29(2): 515–522.

Bawa, Vijay, Stephen Brown, and Roger Klein. 1979. *Estimation Risk and Optimal Portfolio Choice*. Amsterdam: North Holland.

Beale, E. M. L. 1955. "On Minimizing a Convex Function Subject to Linear Inequalities." *Journal of the Royal Statistical Society* (B)17: 173–184.

———— 1959. "On Quadratic Programming." *Naval Research Logistics Quarterly,* 6(3): 227–243.

Berk, Jonathan B. 1995. "A Critique of Size Related Anomalies." *Review of Financial Studies* 8(2): 275–286.

Black, Fischer, and Myron Scholes. 1973. "The Pricing of Options and Corporate Liabilities." *Journal of Political Economy* 81(3): 637–654.

———— and Robert Litterman. 1992. "Global Portfolio Optimization." *Financial Analysts Journal* 48(5): 28–43.

Boyd, S., and L. Vandenberghe. 2004. *Convex Optimization*. Cambridge: Cambridge University Press.

Brinson, Gary, L. Randolph Hood, and Gil Beebower. 1986. "Determinants of Portfolio Performance." *Financial Analyst Journal* 42(4): 39–44.

Brinson, G., B. Singer, and G. Beebower. 1991. "Determinants of Portfolio Performance II: An Update." *Financial Analysts Journal* 47(3): 40–48.

Britten-Jones, M. 1999. "Sampling Error in Mean-Variance Efficient Portfolio Weights." *Journal of Finance* 54(2): 655–671.

Brown, Stephen. 1976. "Optimal Portfolio Choice under Uncertainty." Unpublished Ph.D. dissertation, University of Chicago.

Carlin, Bradley, and Thomas Louis. 1992. *Bayes and Empirical Bayes Methods for Data Analysis.* Boca Raton, FL: Chapman & Hall/CRC.

Ceria, S., and R. Stubbs. 2005. *Incorporating Estimation Error into Portfolio Selection: Robust Efficient Frontiers.* Axioma Working Paper.

Chopra, Vijay. 1991. "Mean-Variance Revisited: Near-Optimal Portfolios and Sensitivity to Input Variations." *Russell Research Commentary* (December).

Chopra, V., and W. Ziemba. 1993. "The Effect of Errors in Means, Variances, and Covariances on Optimal Portfolio Choice." *Journal of Portfolio Management* 19(1): 6–11.

Clarke, R., H. deSilva, and S. Thorley. 2002. "Portfolio Constraints and the Fundamental Law of Active Management." *Financial Analysts Journal* 58(3): 48–66.

Clarke, R., H. deSilva, and S. Thorley. 2006. "The Fundamental Law of Active Portfolio Management." *Journal of Investment Management* 4(3): 54–72.

Copas, J. B. 1983. "Regression Prediction and Shrinkage." *Journal of the Royal Statistical Society* (B)45: 311–354.

DeMiguel, V., L. Garlappi, and R. Uppal. 2006. "1/N." EFA Zurich Meetings, June 22.

Dey, D. K., and C. Srinivasan. 1985. "Estimation of a Covariance Matrix Under Stein's Loss." *Annals of Statistics* 13(4): 1581–1591.

Efron, B. 2005. "Bayesians, Frequentists, and Scientists." *Journal of the American Statistical Association* 100(469): 1–5.

———— and C. Morris. 1973. "Stein's Estimation Rule and Its Competitors—An Empirical Bayes Approach." *Journal of the American Statistical Association* 68(341): 117–130.

———— and C. Morris. 1975. "Data Analysis Using Stein's Estimator and its Generalizations." *Journal of the American Statistical Association* 70(350): 311–319.

———— and C. Morris. 1977. "Stein's Paradox in Statistics." *Scientific American,* 236 (May): 119–127.

———— and Robert Tibshirani. 1993. *An Introduction to the Bootstrap.* New York: Chapman and Hall.

Erlich, Paul. 1997. "Cash Optimization." Acadian Research, Boston, MA. Memo.

Fama, Eugene, and Kenneth French. 1992. "The Cross-Section of Expected Stock Returns." *Journal of Finance* 47(2): 427–465.

Farrell, James L. Jr. 1983. *Guide to Portfolio Management.* McGraw-Hill: 168–174.

Feldman, Barry. 2003. Ibbotson conference presentation.

Frank, M., and P. Wolfe. 1956. "An Algorithm for Quadratic Programming." *Naval Research Logistics Quarterly* 3: 95–110.

Frost, P., and J. Savarino. 1986. "An Empirical Bayes Approach to Efficient Portfolio Selection." *Journal of Financial and Quantitative Analysis* 21(3): 293–305.

———— 1988. "For Better Performance: Constrain Portfolio Weights." *Journal of Portfolio Management* 15(1): 29–34.

Grinold, R. 1989. "The Fundamental Law of Active Management." *Journal of Portfolio Management* 15(3): 30–37.

Grinold, Richard, and Ronald Kahn. 1994. *Active Portfolio Management.* Chicago: Irwin.

Hakansson, Nils. 1971a. "Capital Growth and the Mean-Variance Approach to Portfolio Selection." *Journal of Financial and Quantitative Analysis* 6(1): 517–557.

———— 1971b. "Multi-Period Mean-Variance Analysis: Towards a General Theory of Portfolio Choice." *Journal of Finance* 26(4): 857–884.

Harvey, C., J. Liechty, M. Liechty, and P. Müller. 2003. "Portfolio Selection with Higher Moments." Duke University, Working Paper, (October 16).

Hensel, Chris D., Don Ezra, and John Ilkiw. 1991. "The Importance of the Asset Allocation Decision." *Financial Analyst Journal* 47(4): 65–72.

Jacobs, B., K. Levy, and H. Markowitz. 2006a. "Trimability and Fast Optimization of Long-Short Portfolios." *Financial Analysts Journal* 62(2): 22–34.

Jacobs, B. and K. Levy. 2006b. "Enhanced Active Equity Strategies." *Journal of Portfolio Management* 32(3): 45–55.

James, W., and C. Stein. 1961. "Estimation with Quadratic Loss." *Proceedings of the 4th Berkeley Symposium on Probability and Statistics.* Berkeley: University of California Press, 361–379.

Jobson, J. D. 1991. "Confidence Regions for the Mean-Variance Efficient Set: An Alternative Approach to Estimation Risk." *Review of Quantitative Finance and Accounting* 1: 235–257.

———— and Bob Korkie. 1980. "Estimation for Markowitz Efficient Portfolios." *Journal of the American Statistical Association* 75(371): 544–554.

———— and Bob Korkie. 1981. "Putting Markowitz Theory to Work." *Journal of Portfolio Management* 7(4): 70–74.

———— and Bob Korkie. 1985. "Statistical Inference in Two Parameter Portfolio Theory with Multiple Regression Software." *Journal of Financial and Quantitative Analysis* 18(2): 189–197.

————, Bob Korkie, and Vinod Ratti. 1979. "Improved Estimation for Markowitz Efficient Portfolios Using James-Stein Type Estimators." In *Proceedings of the Business and Economics Statistics Section* in Washington D.C., August 13–16, by the American Statistical Association, 279–284.

————, Bob Korkie, and Vinod Ratti. 1980. "Improved Estimation and Selection Rules for Markowitz Portfolios." *Proceedings of the Annual Meeting of the Western Finance Association.*

Johnson, Richard, and Dean Wichern. 1992. *Applied Multivariate Statistical Analysis,* 3rd ed. Saddle River, NJ: Prentice-Hall.

Jorion, Philippe. 1986. "Bayes-Stein Estimation for Portfolio Analysis." *Journal of Financial and Quantitative Analysis* 21(3): 279–292.

———— 1992. "Portfolio Optimization in Practice." *Financial Analysts Journal* 48(1): 68–74.

———— 1996. Personal communication. Phone.

Judge, George, R. Carter Hill, William Griffiths, Helmut Lutkepohl, and Tsoung-Chao Lee. 1988. *Introduction to the Theory and Practice of Econometrics,* 2nd ed. New York: Wiley.

Kandel, Shmuel, and Robert Stambaugh. 1995. "Portfolio Inefficiency and the Cross-section of Expected Returns." *Journal of Finance* 50(1): 157–184.

Knight, J., and S. Satchell. 2006. "Exact Properties of Measures of Optimal Investment for Institutional Investors." Presented to The Centre for Advanced Studies in Finance and The Institute for Quantitative Finance and Insurance, March.

Kroll, Yoram, Haim Levy, and Harry Markowitz. 1984. "Mean-Variance Versus Direct Utility Maximization." *Journal of Finance* 39(1): 47–61.

Ledoit, Olivier. 1994. "Portfolio Selection: Improved Covariance Matrix Estimation." Sloan School of Management, Working paper (November).

——— 1997. "Improved Estimation of the Covariance Matrix of Stock Returns with an Application to Portfolio Selection." Anderson Graduate School of Management at UCLA, Working paper (March).

Levy, Haim, and Harry Markowitz. 1979. "Approximating Expected Utility by a Function of the Mean and Variance." *American Economic Review* 69(3): 308–317.

Liebowitz, Martin. 1986. "The Dedicated Bond Portfolio in Pension Funds, Part I: Motivations and Basics; Part II: Immuization, Horizon Matching and Contingent Procedures." *Financial Analysts Journal* 42(1): 69–75; 42(2):47–57.

Lintner, John. 1965. "The Valuation of Risk Assets and the Selection of Risky Investments in Stock Portfolios and Capital Budgets." *Review of Economics and Statistics* 47(1): 13–37.

Markowitz, Harry. 1956. "The Optimization of a Quadratic Function Subject to Linear Constraints." *Naval Research Logistics Quarterly* 3(1/2): 111–133.

——— 1959. *Portfolio Selection: Efficient Diversification of Investments.* New York: Wiley, 2nd ed. Cambridge, MA: Basil Blackwell, 1991.

——— 1976. "Investment for the Long-Run: New Evidence for an Old Rule." *Journal of Finance* 31(5): 1273–1286.

——— 1987. Mean-Variance Analysis in Portfolio Choice and Capital Markets. Cambridge, MA: Blackwell.

——— 2005. "Market Efficiency: A Theoretical Distinction and So What?" *Financial Analysts Journal* 61(5): 17–30.

——— and N. Usmen. 2003. "Resampled Frontiers Versus Diffuse Bayes: An Experiment." *Journal of Investment Management* 1(4): 9–25.

Merton, Robert C. 1973. "Theory of Rational Option Pricing" *Bell Journal of Economics and Management Science* 4(1): 141–183.

——— 1987. "Presidential Address: A Simple Model of Capital Market Equilibrium With Incomplete Information." *Journal of Finance* 42(3): 483–510.

Michaud, Richard. 1976. "Pension Fund Investment Policy." Presented to the Institute for Quantitative Research in Finance, Spring Seminar.

——— 1981. "Risk Policy and Long-Term Investment." *Journal of Financial and Quantitative Analysis* 16(2): 147–167.

——— 1989a. "The Markowitz Optimization Enigma: Is Optimized Optimal?" *Financial Analysts Journal* 45(1): 31–42.

——— 1989b. "Economic Surplus and Pension Asset Management." *Merrill Lynch Pension Executive Review* 2(1): 7–13.

——— 1989c. "Pension Policy and Benchmark Optimization." *Investment Management Review* 3(8): 25–30.

——— 1993. "Are Long-Short Equity Strategies Superior?" *Financial Analysts Journal* 49(6): 44–49.

———— 1998. *Efficient Asset Management: A Practical Guide to Stock Portfolio Optimization and Asset Allocation.* Boston: Harvard Business School Press.

———— 1999. *Investment Styles, Market Anomalies, and Global Stock Selection.* Charlottesville, VA: The Research Foundation of the Institute of Chartered Financial Analysts.

———— 2003. "A Practical Framework for Portfolio Choice." *Journal of Investment Management*, 2nd Quarter.

———— and James Monahan. 1981. "Comparisons of Optimal versus Stationary Investment Policies over Time." Presented to the Institute for Quantitative Research in Finance, Spring Seminar.

———— and Paul Davis. 1982. "Valuation Model Bias and the Scale Structure of Dividend Discount Returns." *Journal of Finance* 37(2): 563–573.

———— and Robert Michaud. 2003. "Optimal and Investable Portfolios." *New Frontier Advisors Newsletter* (June).

———— and Robert Michaud. 2004a. "Forecast Confidence Level and Portfolio Optimization." *New Frontier Advisors Newsletter* (July).

———— and Robert Michaud. 2004b. "Equity Optimization Issues - I." *New Frontier Advisors Newsletter* (November).

———— and Robert Michaud. 2005a. "Insignificant Alphas and Heterogeneous Errors." *New Frontier Advisors Newsletter* (March).

———— and Robert Michaud. 2005b. "Fundamental Law of Mismanagement." *New Frontier Advisors Newsletter* (July).

————, Robert Michaud, and Katharine Pulvermacher. 2006a. *Gold as a Strategic Asset.* London: World Gold Council.

———— and Matthew Pierce. 2006b. "Risk-Returns for Strategic Financial Planning." Prepared for AssetMark Investment Services. September.

Michaud, Robert, and Richard Michaud. 2002. "Resampled Portfolio Rebalancing and Monitoring." *New Frontier Advisors Newsletter* (4th quarter).

Perold, Andre. 1984. "Large Scale Portfolio Optimization." *Management Science* 30(10): 1143–1160.

Roll, Richard. 1979. "Testing a Portfolio of Ex Ante Mean-Variance Efficiency" *TIMS Studies in the Management Studies* 11: 135–149.

———— 1992. "A Mean/Variance Analysis of Tracking Error." *Journal of Portfolio Management* 18(4): 13–22.

———— and Stephen Ross. 1994. "On the Cross-Sectional Relation Between Expected Returns and Betas." *Journal of Finance* 49(1): 101–121.

Rosenberg, Barr. 1974. "Extra-Market Components of Covariance in Security Returns." *Journal of Financial and Quantitative Analysis* March 9(2): 263–273.

Rosenberg, Barr, and Walt McKibben. 1973. "The Prediction of Systematic and Specific Risk in Common Stocks." *Journal of Financial and Quantitative Analysis* 8(3): 317–333.

———— and James Guy. 1973. "Beta and Investment Fundamentals." *Financial Analysts Journal* 32(3): 60–72; 32(4): 62–70.

Ross, Stephen. 1975. "Return, Risk and Arbitrage." In *Studies in Risk and Return*, edited by I. Friend and J. Bicksler. Cambridge, MA: Ballinger.

———— 1976. "The Arbitrage Theory of Capital Asset Pricing." *Journal of Economic Theory* 13(3): 341–360.

Rubinstein, Mark. 1973. "A Comparative Statics Analysis of Risk Premiums." *Journal of Business* 46(4): 605–615.

Shanken, Jay. 1985. "Multivariate Tests of the Zero-Beta CAPM." *Journal of Financial Economics* 14(3): 327–357.

——— 1992. "The Current State of the Arbitrage Pricing Theory." *Journal of Finance* 47(4): 1569–1574.

——— 1996. "Statistical Methods in Tests of Portfolio Efficiency: A Synthesis." In *Handbook of Statistics,* vol. 14, edited by G. S. Maddala and C. R. Rao. Amsterdam: Elsevier.

Sharpe, William. 1963. "A Simplified Model for Portfolio Analysis." *Management Science* 9(2): 277–293.

——— 1964. "Capital Asset Prices: A Theory of Market Equilibrium Under Conditions of Risk." *Journal of Finance* 19(3): 425–442.

——— 1970. *Portfolio Theory and Capital Markets.* New York: McGraw-Hill.

——— 1985. *Investments.* Englewood Cliffs, NJ: Prentice-Hall, 666–670.

——— 1992. "Asset Allocation: Management Style and Performance Measurement." *Journal of Portfolio Management* 18(1): 7–19.

Stein, C. 1955. "Inadmissibility of the Usual Estimator of the Mean of a Multivariate Normal Distribution." *Proceedings of the 3rd Berkeley Symposium on Probability and Statistics.* Berkeley: University of California Press.

——— 1982. Series of lectures given at the University of Washington, Seattle.

Theil, Henri. 1971. *Principles of Econometrics.* New York: Wiley: 282–293.

——— and A.S. Goldberger. 1961. "On Pure and Mixed Statistical Estimation in Economics." *International Economic Review* 2(1): 65–78.

Wolfe, P. 1959. "The Simplex Algorithm for Quadratic Programming." *Econometrica* 27(3): 382–398.

Young, William, and Robert Trent. 1969. "Geometric Mean Approximations of Individual Security and Portfolio Performance." *Journal of Financial and Quantitative Analysis* 4(2): 179–199.

Index